UNDERGROUND
ALIEN
BASES

COMMANDER X

ABELARD PRODUCTIONS, INC.

UNDERGROUND ALIEN BASES

First printing 1990
Special Limited Edition

© 1990 by
ABELARD PRODUCTIONS, INC.

Graphics by Cosmic Computerized Systems, Inc.

CONTENTS

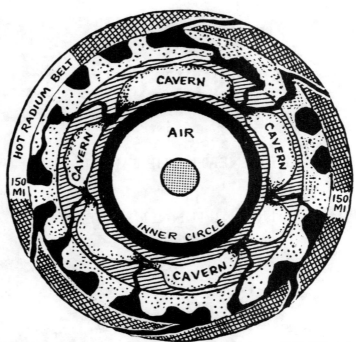

Ancient teachings claim that a great "Cavern World" exists inside the Earth and that there are 1,400 mile openings at both the North and South Poles.

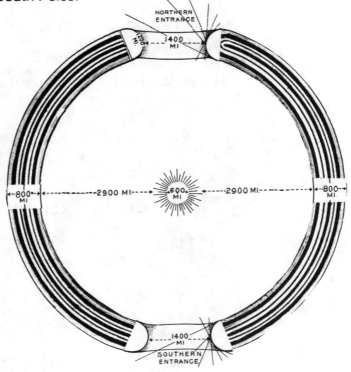

Life Beneath
The Earth's Surface

Way back in the late 1940s, it was apparent that some pretty disturbing things were happening in the sky above us.

Reports of silvery discs flashing in the noon sun became common occurrences as people from all walks of life—from all over the world—came forward to tell of their sightings of what were called "flying saucers," and then UFOs.

Little by little, the intensity of the reports began to heat up.

Not only were pilots and other trained observers being chased by these craft that shouldn't have been parading around, but our own military began to take an active interest in this "weirdness" that seemed to defy the very laws of science. Those willing to climb out on a limb and tell about what they were a party to, often found themselves the center of unnecessary hostility. Some witnesses lost their jobs, their homes, their wives (or husbands)...and a few may have even lost their lives!

Initially, there was some speculation that these objects might have been manufactured by some Earthly government. After all, during World War II, Hitler and his Nazi scientists were known to be working on a variety of rockets and missiles, some of which were definitely circular in shape. Little by little, this theory for the origin of UFOs began to be played down as captured documents showed that the Nazis were just as dazed and confused as the Americans were in regard to the "fly over" of these strange and very unearthly craft.

In the late 1940s and early 50s, a writer by the name of Major Donald E. Keyhoe helped popularize the space ship theme for the first time, though if researchers had bothered to study already existing records, they would have discovered at least one other writer, Charles Fort, had in the 1920s already compiled a pretty large file of data detailing hundreds of reports from around the globe...some as early as the eighteen hundreds—and before!

As humankind reached out to the planets, it became obvious that intelligent life as we know it did not likely live on any of the planets in our own solar system. Venus and Mercury are way too hot, while the worlds beyond Mars get little sunlight and would certainly have to be as cold as hell.

This is not to say that other forms of life don't exist all around us.

The legends and folklore of all races have long told of "invisible worlds" and beings from "higher planes" who have visited Earth to offer guidance and comfort since the very beginning of humankind. In fact, there is a large body of evidence which says that these beings—of all shapes, sizes, and forms—helped in our development, perhaps even "seeding" the planet with flesh and blood, physical beings. The American Indians, for example, tell of the "Sky Gods" who came down and mingled with them, helping with the planting and giving advice when needed. Even before, the Egyptians, the Incas and the Aztecs might have also found themselves playing "host" to "strangers from afar." And let's not forget the stories told in the Bible of "angels" who materialized from time after time to foster a rather complex belief system that is now followed by millions of Christians worldwide.

Where do the majority of UFOs, aliens, and the other beings we know "little about" come from?

It seems almost out of the question to think that they would travel millions of miles each day to stop off and abduct a human or two; or draw power from one of our high-tension lines; or—for that matter—to give an airline or fighter pilot the scare of their life.

Chances are that Paulo J. Strauss, a Commander of the Brazilian Navy, was correct when he stated the following:

"One should not ignore the legends of enchanted cities (under the Earth)...I believe these mysterious apparatuses (UFOs) come from inside the Earth, where it has long been believed that life exists to a degree far advanced over our own civilization."

A theory held by only a few researchers over the years (such as the late Raymond Palmer, editor of Search, Amazing Stories, Fate and Flying Saucers), very recent confirmatiion of such an amazing idea has come from the likes of John Lear, William Hamilton III, and Bill Cooper, who have spoken at length about the existence of underground bases at various locations throughout North America, particularly at Dulce, New Mexico, where aliens have taken over the lower levels of the military base there. It is at Dulce that a negative group of aliens, best known as the "Greys" or the "EBEs" have established a fortress, spreading out to other parts of the U.S. via means of a vast underground tunnel system that has virtually existed before recorded history, and which has been "improved upon" by the original descendants of Atlantis, as well as other groups who now survive and go about their business unknown to the majority of us living on the Earth's surface.

From my own intelligence work with the military, I can say with all certainty that one of the main reasons the public has been kept in total darkness about the reality of UFOs and aliens, is that the truth of the matter actually exists too close to home to do anything about. How could a spokesman for the Pentagon dare admit that five or ten thousand feet underground exists an entire world that is "foreign" to a belief structure we have had for centuries? How could, for example, our fastest bomber be any challenge to these aerial invaders when we can only guess about the routes they take to the surface; eluding radar as they fly so low, headed back to their underground liar?

Yes, it is true that many space crews are arriving here regularly from other planets located in far away galaxies, but those that have a real reason for arriving at our cosmic shores can be said to be recent subterranean immigrants, using underground bases as a "way station." Some of these beings have our best interests at heart; some are neutral in their standing while others are out to take all they can, plundering our planet of riches, abducting humans for their own bizarre purposes, and wreaking havoc in every way possible. Unfortunately, some of these beings are being helped by still other "undergrounders" who are native to the caves and tunnels of Earth.

Cosmic Awareness

Believe me, I am the first to demand "documentation" and "physical evidence" before accepting anything wholeheartedly, but while with the military on various occasions, I was privileged to witness a variety of "paranormal phenomena" involving mind control, telepathy and channeling, which I can only describe as "utterly astonishing." It is common knowledge that astronaut Edgar Mitchell, while on the moon, attempted to pick up thoughts from a clairvoyant operating out of a laboratory in Chicago. It may not be known, however, that several times psychics have been used—and I must say successfully!—to converse with space beings. Some of these channels or mediums have been private citizens, but in my previous book—*The Ultimate Deception*—I wrote about the case of a CIA agent who was actually used in an experiment to contact aliens...going so far as having them put on a "show" outside the Pentagon.

Many have placed Paul Shockley in the same league as the late Edgar Cayce. The accuracy of this "trance interpreter" is said to be "uncanny," as he zeros in on extraordinary matters. The following information on the nature of the Underground World we walk over every day, has been communicated through certain carefully-trained channels under his tutelage and has been derived from deep, super-conscious trance states. What I like most about Mr. Shockley's work—as opposed to other channelers who say we *must* accept every world they utter—is that Paul's "masters" teach us not to believe anything, "but to question, explore, doubt and discover for yourself, through your own channel, what is truth." I feel strongly that we have a better chance to understand what is really going on as far as alien bases go, after consulting this very remarkable source, who may be reached through: Cosmic Awareness, Box 115, Olympia, Washington 98507.

• • •

Thousands of Miles of Tunnels Exist
Beneath the U.S. Where Aliens Exist

"This Awareness indicates that there is an awareness by the United States government of these caves and caverns under the surface of this Earth. Many are in the United States. This Awareness indicates that there is in fact an organization called the '165 Mile Club' which is made up of entities working with the government who have been 165 miles deep into the subterranean caverns. This Awareness indicates that IT wishes to warn entities to stay out of these caves and caverns, as there is grave danger in these, particularly in those which are remote and not visited by tourists. This Awareness indicates that generally those which are known as tourist attractions are not used by these subterranean beings.

"This Awareness indicates that essentially the Earth's surface is catacombed with many tunnels, that there are also areas where there is much hot lava—these areas of course are not used by these beings and the tunnels avoid contact with such areas. This Awareness indicates that there are tunnels running approximately 4,000 miles from the Eastern part of the United States, to an area in Arizona and into areas north to Vancouver, approximately 1,800 miles. This Awareness indicates there are many other branches and caverns coming off these. This Awareness indicates that there are also tunnels in South America, Tibet, in various places in Europe—these running underground. This Awareness indicates there are even tunnels which move beneath the ocean floors, linking the continents together."

Detrimental Robots (Deros) Live Beneath the Earth

"This Awareness indicates that these so-called Deros are also the basis for certain folklore such as gnomes and elves, goblins, trolls. This Awareness indicates that the folklore relating unto these entities has changed somewhat and that many of the so-called gnomes, trolls, elves and imps that many of these are now projected as being nice little fellows. This Awareness suggests that this is a way of reconciling, or healing, or diffusing the fear and hostility and so-called evilness of these entities, so that they may cease to be the garbage can for human hostilities, fears and enemies.

"This Awareness indicates that those so-called Deros, or Detrimental Robots, those entities live beneath the crust of the Earth—this Awareness indicates that there are many types of entities beneath the Earth; that those closer to the center itself are of a highly evolved nature, whereas those who are sub-surface entities, these are somewhat demented by the effects of living underground for so many thousands of years. This Awareness indicates that those Deros, or detrimental robots, or whatever name entities desire, are human beings who have regressed through misuse of power, through excessive and continued self-indulgence, and through greed, lust, competition, and joy in sadistic expressions.

"This Awareness indicates that occasionally these entities sur-

9

face, particularly through certain buildings which are often built in a way to allow an opening into the subterranean levels, and occasionally these entities walk around on the streets of your cities, and occasionally these entities have even been known to kidnap others. This Awareness indicates these entities are not astral beings, are not entities who are being imagined or experienced after death. These entities are as real as you, 'and in this particular dimension of reality which is yours.' This Awareness indicates that these entities are tools of the Alien Force—that the Alien Force expresses through these entities, that they are essentially slaves of the Alien Force, as also are many of the creatures known as Bigfoot, or of the similar types of hairy monsters."

Bigfoot Entities Were Once Highly Evolved

"This Awareness indicates that these Sasquatch-type entities do not care to move too close to humans on the outer surface of the Earth. This Awareness suggests these entities having great karma to work off, yet fully aware of their karma and very lonely entities. This Awareness indicating these entities having a type of consciousness which allow them to know precisely where any other human is within a two mile area of their being and can move away from these humans very easily through that psychic understanding.

"This Awareness indicates these entities as having extremely high beings in that civilization (on the planet Maldek which was destroyed), having great responsibility and misusing that responsibility, and in that misuse did lead to the devastation of that planet. This Awareness indicates this occurring approximately 300,000 years ago. This Awareness indicates that the movement of the entities through states of reincarnation: as these souls moved into the Earth's sphere, these entities were outcast by the rest of consciousness upon this plane and those inner planes within the Earth's sphere; and these entities do live alone with some communication relating unto beings who have greater understanding and who can work with these entities.

"This Awareness indicates that 85% of the souls upon this plane have lived on Maldek and this is the Luciferian consciousness which is being worked off as part of the Earth's karma. This Awareness indicates this as being dissolved. This entire Illuminati, money-changing trip is but a replay of the memory of the action

10

which occurred on Maldek wherein beings were categorized, numbered and enslaved. This Awareness indicates that the movement which began 60,000 years ago in Atlantis was but a recollection of certain states which began on Maldek.

"This Awareness suggests that in reference to Bigfoot entities, these entities understand the terror they instilled in the human creature which walks on the surface of the Earth and therefore, by instinct, avoid these creatures. This Awareness indicates that it is this fear which fascinates and terrorizes the human mind when thinking of the Bigfoot. This Awareness indicates that those entities on the inner plane, deep beneath the Earth's surface, are capable of relating to Bigfoot without such fear and without the type of curiosity and hostility as would be felt by the entities on the surface of this plane.

"This Awareness indicates that it shall eventually become necessary for entities from this plane to release their hostility and their subconscious fears of these entities, and in this action the karma that has been held by these entities shall begin to dissolve, and the lamb shall lie down with the beast and the beast shall find a place of rest in the arms of this Awareness."

Many UFOs Come From Beneath the Earth

"This Awareness indicates that many of the UFOs are from this subterranean level and are piloted by these Deros, or by other mechanical creatures such as the synthetics, which are made from parts of entities or animals such as cattle. This Awareness indicates that the cerebral and nervous systems of cattle are often put into these synthetics and the synthetics then are given life, and are used, are inhabited by astral beings who enter these bodies and serve as owners for those bodies and receive their programming from the Alien Force."

"This Awareness indicates those entities known as MIBs, or Men in Black, which often show up after UFO sightings—these entities also are from this lower region, that these entities also assist the Alien Force. These entities have the capacity to move from one dimension to another, may enter into a physical body from an astral level. This Awareness indicates that these entities are also connected with that which has been described previously as the Illuminati, and that which is the Anti-Christ, and this shall eventually be made more clear to entities as the information surfaces on many levels. This Awareness indicates that this information which has just been given may be withheld for future publication along with other UFO information. This not to be released at this time.

"This Awareness indicates that there are very sinister forces working upon this plane, and within the caverns beneath the surface of the Earth. These forces do need to be understood, but these forces must be understood in a manner whereby they may be disarmed, rather than feared. That it is possible to change the basic motivation of these aliens, that they may rejoin the ranks of the merciful."

An Ancient Tunnel System

There is an ancient tunnel system beneath the Earth that literally circles the globe.

This system has existed beneath our very feet for literally thousands of years and very few of us know about it. And those that do have often found their lives turned into a living hell when they dared try to tell others of its very existence.

The tunnels radiate outward from the Arctic and Antarctic in every direction and cover every continent on the planet. They were constructed by a civilization that existed before the "great flood." This civilization came even before that of Atlantis, though the Atlanteans later improved on this existing system, adding to it, as well as establishing underground space ports for visitors arriving from other planets who came here in those "early days" to establish friendly "trade relations" with our planet's peoples. Sometime in the distant past—after the collapse of Atlantis—these caverns were at first abandoned and then taken over by negative space aliens, who collaborated with a race of our own underground beings (known as the Dero) to rape the planet of all its vital resources. Humans were taken as "slaves" to work in the underground tunnels from which few were ever able to escape. We are told that cities actually exist beneath the Earth's outer crust, and they can be reached by entering and existing through concealed openings in various locations. Most "shaftways" to these inner Earth cities can be found in remote areas, while others are in more populated areas. There is supposedly even an opening somewhere in New York City in the vicinity of midtown Manhattan that can be reached through an abandoned elevator shaft that only a very few know about for obvious "security" reasons.

Confirmation Received

Back in the late 1940s and early 50s a channel by the name of

13

Mark Probert was very popular on the West Coast. Much of the information he received came from the Yada Di Shi'ite, a 50,000 year old Tibetan master who was known to keep a "watchful eye" on happenings on both the physical as well as etheric planes. The Yada confirmed a great deal about the reality of the underground world and even spoke of a race of "Serpent People" who once over-ran this planet, having come here from Venus in the remote past. Says the Yada:

"They abandoned the Earth because conditions here were not favorable to them. They were of great size and had scaly bodies and large frog eyes, and were very advanced mentally. Morally they were not evolved, but were extremely cruel and vicious. They are still to be found in the interior of Venus. The Venusians of the present day, however, are not descendants of this early type.

"Venusians who are visiting your Earth at present want to bring peace. They have no desire to occupy the Earth. There is no present warfare between them and the Martians....

"Your present danger, mitigated for a time by the Guardians (from Venus and elsewhere), lies in the progressive breakdown of the upper ethers, that is, of the ionosphere (which regulates the climate of the globe and shields us from the impact of the cosmic rays.).

"Most of what is said about the tunnel system is correct. These were constructed by Atlanteans, partly for communication, sometimes in connection with the search for metals or ores, but chiefly in order to escape the extreme solar radiation and various bacteria from the surface of the globe. The great plague that visited England (1666 A.D.?), while partly due to unclean living, was mostly caused by these same bacteria.

"The tunnels themselves were not primarily designed for underground living; but in many cases they lead into vast caverns, natural or artificially hollowed out, where a great number of persons spent all their lives. It is true that the tunnel opening under the pyramid of Gizeh in Egypt leads into the caverns under Tibet. As to size, a common diameter of these tunnels was about 150 feet.

"They were constructed by mechanical means or chemical means; that is, by the application of superheat deteriorators. It was like burning their way through the Earth. Yes, it resembled the heat of the atomic bomb—if such heat could be controlled and directed.

It was a very dangerous process; for if the heat blast went out of control the whole globe might suffer most serious consequences. The process was very rapid. The molecules disintegrated. The substances of the Earth are very porous and the gasses were largely absorbed by it.

"In some quarters much is still known about these tunnels. The two great religious Hierarchies of your plane have such knowledge, and in fact have stored great supplies of food in underground depots. They are aware of the approach of their twilight hour."

"So the vast tunnel system dating from Atlantean times, with its hub under a still-lived-in-city in the Antarctic, is known to the lamas and priests of Northern Buddhism, and to the priesthood of the Roman Catholic Church; it is not only known but made use of; and apparently their soothsayers have foreseen a great surface catastrophe, such as that which might be caused by a Polar Flip, and have made preparations accordingly.

"The one God of the world of matter is the god of Change," concluded the Yada. "All things move into and out of Manifestation in the three dimensions. Where does form come from? Mind built it and will change it according to the need for change. The object lost to three dimensions still holds to form another plane. To know this and *know* that we know it, is to escape much sorrow when forms—of cherished things, beloved persons—vanish from the world of our sense perceptions."

The above communication from the Yada was first published in the BSRA *Round Robin* journal of borderland research for March-April, 1953, edited and published by Meade Layne.

• • •

One individual who studied the ancient tunnel system was the late journalist John J. Robinson of Jersey City, New Jersey, who several times was a guest on the popular Long John Nebel talk show heard over radio station WOR in New York. Jack was a student of history who became fascinated with folklore's many legends about the subterranean world beneath our feet. Though many of the stories were of ancient vintage, Jack realized that there was something a lot more complex going on than meets the eye at first glance. After years of careful study and research, and after talking

15

with those with first hand "knowledge," he became convinced that these ancient tunnels were very much a party of today's reality, regardless of if we wanted to accept them as fact or not. Several of John Robinson's journals recently fell into my hands, and I am thus able to report on his personal findings concerning these tunnels in several areas of the globe.

Tunnels of South America

In Southern and Central America as well as in Mexico, the ancient people did not deny the presence or existence of subterranean caves, chambers or tunnels. An examination of the religious beliefs of all these ancient civilizations will reveal this.

The Aztec of Mexico had their dark, dreary and much feared "Tlalxico" which was ruled by "Mictlan," their god of death. The Mayas of Yucatan held a belief in the existence of nine underworlds. These they termed "Mitlan" and they were icy cold as are most subterranean chambers or tunnels. (For proof visit a large cavern in summer clothes and see how uncomfortable you are.) These underworlds were presided over by "Ah Puch," the Lord of Death. We also have mention of the underground in the Mayan sacred writings, the "Popol Veh;" as well as in the *Book of Chilam Balam of Chumayel*. Even some of the codices seem to refer to them.

Peru and Chile, when they were ruled by the Incas, also reveal knowledge of the underground. "Supai," the god of death, had an underground dwelling, a much feared "Place of Darkness." "Pachacamce," the god of the Earth, caused underground rumbles in subterranean places where huge stones evidently fell, hours after he had shaken the Earth with violence.

A legend of the first Inca "Manco Capac" related that he and his followers, the founders of the Inca realm, came from underground caves. While the people of the time revered snakes because of "Urcaguay" the god of underground treasures. This god is depicted as a large snake whose tail has hanging pendant from it the head of a deer and many little gold chains. Even the "Comentarios Reales de los Incas" of Garciliasso de la Vega, hints at the existence of the subterranean.

References to the tunnels have come down to us from information that the conquistadores obtained. From some unknown source

16

they had gathered information that the wealth of the Incas domain was stored in a vast underground tunnel or road. Pizarro held the Inca Atahuelpha prisoner in order to obtain his wealth. Wealth which it was rumored was stored in a vast subterranean tunnel that ran for many miles below the surface of the Earth. The Inca, if he had the information regarding the entrance to this tunnel, never revealed it. The priests of the Sun god and the Inca's wife determined, it is asserted, the eventual fate of the Inca, by occult means. The knowledge that Pizarro did not intend to spare the Inca Atahuelphas life caused them to seal up the entrance and hide it so well that it has never been found to this day.

A few Quicha Indians, who are pure descendants of the line of priests still have the knowledge of the location, of the entrance to this tunnel. They are the appointed guardians of this secret, at least so it is rumored today in Peru.

Another source of tunnel information may be a huge monolith of perpendicular rock, which stands apart from its native habitat, the mountains. This rock is of lava, how it was erected or who erected it is lost in the ages of antiquity, long before the Incas came on the scene. The huge monolith stands alone on the shore at Ila, a small town in the southern tip of Peru, not far from the Chilean border. The rock bears odd hieroglyphic marks carved upon it; marks which only in the setting sun's light create a cryptic group of symbols—symbols which may be viewed through the lens of a field glass. It is said that these marks will reveal to the person able to read them and decipher the message correctly the location of a secret entrance to the tunnels. An entrance located, some researchers assert, in the fastness of the "Los Tres Picas," the Three Peaks region. This is a triangular formation of mountain tops situated near the monolity in the Loa River section.

When Mme. Blavatsky visited Peru, she viewed the concurred with the information regarding the markings on the Ila monolith. She also asserted that information regarding the entrances to the tunnels had been graven in the walls of the "Sun Temple" at Cusco. Information of a symbolized nature, but nevertheless information which revealed to the person with the knowledge of the meaning of the symbols, the secret entrances to those tunnels which the priests of the "Sun God" knew about. It is reported that Mme. Blavatsky received a chart of the tunnels, from an old Indian, when she visited

Lima; a chart which now reposes in the Adyar, India, archives of the Theosophical Society.

Harold T. Wilkins, author of *Mysteries of Ancient South America,* also researched and inquired about the tunnels until he was able to conclude the following: Two underground roads leave the vicinity of Lima, Peru. One of these tunnels is a subterranean road to Cusco, almost 400 miles to the east. The other runs underground in a southern direction for over 900 miles to the vicinity of Salar de Atacama. This is the large salt desert in Chile. It is the residue of the ocean water which was landlocked during an upheaval of the Earth. The upheaval or cataclysm which created Lake Titicaca and raised Huanuco high above its place on the shore line, creating the Andes and a new shore line on the west coast of South America. (For information regarding this event, see the section titled "Tiahuanacu in the Andes" in Immanuel Velikovsky's *Earth in Upheaval.*)

The Cordellerias Domeyko in that section of Chile very evidently landlocked a great portion of the sea when it was raised. After the sea water evaporated the vast salt waste, which is almost impossible to traverse, was left.

The tunnel, which has an entrance somewhere in the Los Tres Picos triangle, is also said to have a connection with this long southern underground road.

I conjecture that any continuation of southern tunnel was broken during the cataclysm which created the Andian mountain range. Such a continuation would have connected these ancient tunnels with the reputed Rainbow City center in the Antarctic.

I also conjecture that another event may have also happened during the shifting of the Earth's crust at that time. Some of my readers may be familiar with the fact that at lest one tribe of Indians in the southwestern United States have a legend of coming from South America.

This legend relates a story of many years ago. The forefathers of the tribe are said to have lived in a large city far to the south. The story even ties the stars in the sky with the Southern Cross. The town may have been Huanaca before the Earth shift which raised it above sea level. At any rate, the legend asserts that the people of this town in the south, the forefathers of a tribe of American Indians, were driven from their home in order to escape the depreda-

18

tions and attacks of a much more hostile and fierce group of warriors. The remnants of those who fled wandered for a long, long time in underground passages which led to the north. These passages eventually led them to our southwest, where they emerged and set up tribal life once again.

How these ancient Indians were able to see in the dark does not seem to have been taken into consideration. The question of how these ancient tunnels of the Atlan or Titian were illuminated has long been of interest to those interested in the Shaver mystery. It has long been considered that the tunnels were lit by a type of atomic light.

Steve Brodie is once again a captive, if he is still alive! I cannot ask him about this and I regret that I did not speak to him about this when I did talk with him. I do know, however, that he never mentioned darkness except in relation to the weird outer space pictures he painted. Light is a funny thing. We accept it as our due and never notice it until it is missing. Perhaps some time in the future we may find one of the entrances to the caves and discover just how they are lit.

While I was composing this article, Dominick Lucchesi called to see me. "Dom" is a very close friend and fellow research associate in matters of "Flying Saucers" and the "Shaver Mystery." He also is one of that very small group known as the "Gray Barker Team." However "Dom" may best be recognized by those in saucer research because of the part he played in the "Bender mystery"; while "Shaver" fans may well recall his "Dero" broadcasts on radio station WOR with Long John Nebel.

Those who have read Gary Barker's book, *They Knew Too Much About Flying Saucers,* will remember that it was Lucchesi who visited Al Bender and to whom Gray dedicated the book to— Dom along with August C. Roberts—whom Barker's book is also dedicated to—when to Bridgeport, Connecticut and questioned Al in regards to the events which made him close down his active saucer group. Bender, as many well know, related his startling solution in a book which Barker published himself, entitled *Flying Saucers & The Three Men.*

Dom has experimented for many years with electronic gadgets, building many radio transmitters and receivers. He holds an amateur radio license for the experimental 6 meter band. He has also built devices which might be able to pick up signals from UFO.

Dom also began to build experimental miniaturized versions of metal locators. His research in this field has also led him to a study of treasure maps. This study also led to the discovery of a very secret group known as "Kafan" or the "Circle of Companions," who are active in the field of treasure hunting. The Kafan hunt treasure very secretly and should they find it they merely remove it and replace everything exactly as it was before they arrived. Then can then convert the treasure, with no one the wiser.

The reason for Dom's visit was his startling news, and to prove it he brought with him a pencil copy of the "Lue" map for me to see. The "Lue" treasure map is nothing like a cartographical map. It is a cryptograph the symbols of which are said to reveal the location of many ancient treasures. It is claimed that only two people have ever managed to decipher this map and both of these are very wealthy.

Dom felt sure that he has managed to decipher the symbols of this cryptograph and from what he showed me, I also feel that he has. If this ancient map reveals that I think it does, some tunnel entrances are revealed in its symbolism as well as a good many other treasures. The only trouble may be that the Kafan could have been there before the seeker. The map is said to be the work of the "Layayam," but to me this may well be the ancient Atlantean.

The Nahanni Valley

The Nahanni Valley is a warm mist-covered valley of an area which covers close to 250 square miles. It is located in the southern end of the Mackenzie Mountains of Canada. It also lies almost 550 miles due west of Fort Simpson on the Mackenzie River of northwest Canada.

This portion of northwest Canada is above 60° latitude which is in the same latitude as is the Yukon Territory. This portion of the northland becomes very cold in the winter, however the valley never becomes as cold as the surrounding country. Hot springs and sulphur geysers are plentiful in the valley; therefore, the valley is covered by mist, while the temperature always remains at least a good 30° above normal. The foliage and trees in the valley remain verdant during the entire year, while the growth is heavier than in the surrounding section.

20

Strange as it may seem, this warm area in a region which becomes bitter cold is not inhabited by anything but the animals who seek warmth during those cold winter months. Even though the valley is rich in fur-bearing animals, it is reported that trappers will not follow the animals into or trap in this valley.

The Indian tribes of the area avoid it and the list is an impressive one, for it includes the Ojibways, the Slave, the Dogribs, the Stoney, the Beavers and the Chipweyans.

The Nahanni Valley, my readers must understand, is not a veritable tropical paradise in the midst of the white wastes of Canada. No prehistoric monsters, leftovers from the Cretaceous or Jurassic periods of the late Mesozoic age, roam this section. Pterodactyl do not soar above it nor do Coelacanths reside in the run-offs of the host springs and geysers. No Neanderthal or Cro-Magnon men are resident, the Yeti (Abominable Snowmen), Bigfoot nor the Sasquatch do not haunt this valley. Legends have so claimed, but none have ever been seen. True, huge footprints have been found imprinted in the former sandy soil which is now shale and in other type of prehistoric rock—but there were giants on the Earth then. The Elders!

Why then do the humans who live near this valley not take advantage of its warmth, as the animals do, why do humans eschew its comfort in the cold winter months?

Because of one reason the valley is known as "The Valley of Headless Men." Although no one or anything has been seen in this valley, those who were foolhardy enough to enter it in search of gold—which is said to be in the valley—have been found by various search parties (who were never molested) as cadavers minus their heads—or should I state as skeletons minus a skull.

A few very bold white fur hunters have gone into the valley and returned with a rich catch. They could never be persuaded to return the second time. They said that the utter loneliness of the country, the eternal mists, which made you see things which were not there along with the feeling that something was watching you, was just too much to take again. The Indians cannot be persuaded to enter the valley, they act as if there were some unseen and unknown forces in it which it was best to fear.

Some headstrong and now headless seekers of gold have entered this valley. The list of those who lost their heads over the gold in the Nahanni Valley is as follows: two brothers, William and Frank Macleod, John Potter, a prospector who was strong, tough, and experienced—he was found a year later by a search party, minus his head, with an exploded cartridge in the rifle, which the bones of his hand still clutched. Examination showed that he had not starved to death, for he still had a cache of food. He had merely lost the means of ingesting it. Later a fearless sourdough came from the Yukon Territory. Undaunted by the tales of danger, he set off into the valley. When he had not returned after two years, a search party located his remains, minus a head, with cans of food in a knapsack.

Two more men who entered the valley at later dates have also been found by searching parties, both as headless corpses. One thing which stands out in all the deaths which have occurred in this valley is that those persons who entered the valley in search of anything which related to the Earth or under the Earth have been found decapitated. Search parties and bold trappers who were not interested in anything which lay below the surface were not molested.

There is something in this valley which the Indians fear—some unknown something which relates to the underground, which maintains the secrecy of "The Valley of the Headless Men."

Liyobaa Cave Entrance

After the conquest of South America by the Spanish conquistadores, the Catholic priests who were attempting to convert the heathen Indians, discovered this entrance to what they called "Hell." This entrance has since been sealed off with tons of rubble, dirt and large stones and boulders.

The village of "Liyobaa" or to translate, "The Cavern of Death," was located in the province of Zapoteca, somewhere near the ancient village of "Mictlan" or the village of the "Underworld."

The Cavern of Death was actually located in the last chamber of an eight chamber building or temple. This temple had four rooms above the ground and four more important chambers built below the surface of the Earth. The High Priests of the then-prevailing Indian religion conducted the ordinary ceremonies for the common man of Theozapotlan in the upper rooms. It was when they descended into the subsurface chambers that the secret and, to them, holy ceremonies, were conducted.

The first underground room was the one which was reserved for any human sacrifice, its walls were lined with the images of the representations of their various "Gods." A blood-stained stone altar in the center of the chamber served for the sacrifice of any human victim, whose still-beating heart would be torn from a screaming still-living body and offered to the lips of those same stone idols for their supposed repletion.

There was a second door in this first chamber which led to the second room. This was a crypt where the preserved bodies of all the deceased high priests reposed. The next door in this crypt led to the third underground vault about the walls of which were the preserved bodies of all the former "Kings" of Theozapotlan. For on the death of a king his body was brought to this chamber and installed there with all the state and glory as well as with many sacrifices to accompany him.

It was from this burial chamber of kings that the fourth and last underground room was accessible. A doorway in this third room led into the last underground chamber which seems appropriately to have contained nothing but another entrance to either *hell* or the *caves* should be covered but unencumbered in the area about it for the benefit of those who wish to leave rapidly and wisely. The huge stone slab covered the entrance in this room to the Temple itself, the doorway to the "Cavern of Death." It was conceived by the Catholic Fathers of that day that this was an entrance to Hades. However, we may well understand it was an entrance to a Dero larder.

Through this doorway, behind the stone slab, was placed the bodies of all human sacrifices as well as the bodies of all the great lords and chieftains of the land who fell in battle. The bodies of these warriors were brought from far and near to be thrown into this cave when they had been cut down in the warfare which was constantly being waged by these people. Many of the common people, when debilitated by an incurable illness or oppressed by an unsupportable hardship, which made them seek death, would prevail upon the high priests to allow them to enter the door of death while still living. They believed that if they did so they would be the recipients of a very special afterlife.

The high priests would sometimes accept them as a living sacrifice and after special ceremonies allow them to enter the "Cavern of Death," while still living. Needless to say, none ever returned to describe their visits.

The Catholic Priests, in order to convert the believers in this myth to Christianity, made arrangements to enter this subterranean door with a large retinue of torch holders and a long rope, which was tied to the stone slab door. They also took the precaution of having a large armed guard make sure that the door was not closed on them.

Entering into this passage they found that they had to descend a number of large steps. At the foot of these steps were the bones of recent arrivals which looked as if they had been picked clean of all flesh. They noticed that a set of huge stone pillars seemed to hold up the very mountain they knew they were beneath. As they advanced, dark air assailed their nostrils, serpents retreated from the light of their torches and at times they seemed to see distorted figures retreat from the light behind the shadow of the pillars in the distance.

They continued into the depths for about the distance of 40 meters when suddenly a strong cold wind began to blow about them seeming to come from everywhere. Still striving to continue as the torches were extinguished rapidly, they took flight when all became dark, not only from fear of serpents, but also strange sounds they could not identify. When all the company had swiftly retreated to the outer chamber of "Hell," they quickly sealed the slab door for all time.

The Maltese Cave Entrance

The Maltese cave entrance is located in the island of Malta. This island is the largest of a group of three and is located in the Mediterranean, dividing Europe from Africa. They lay well of the coast of a much larger island named Sicily, halfway between the Libyan seaport of Tripoli and the Calabria of Italy's Calabrese people, who are located in the toe of the bootlike formation of Italy.

The three Maltese islands are composed of Gozo, Comino and Malta. They are one of the smallest archipelagoes in the world, survivors of those remote days when continents were of a different shape. Those pre-cataclysm days when Atlantis and Mu may have existed, the days when there was a land bridge between Europe and Africa; those days when the entire Mediterranean area was merely a series of large lakes.

Malta is the principal island of the three, for it reaches a width almost nine miles while it is all of seven-and-a-half miles in length. Gozo is not as long as Malta is wide and Comino is almost a dot which separates them. Comino has at times boasted of a total population of 50 people.

The large island Malta is the most southern one for it is only 180 miles from the African coast. It was an ancient center of civilization at the time when the Phoenicians from Carthage invaded and began to rule it. At that time blood sacrifice was not new to the Maltese and they readily accepted the priests of Moloch, which is another name for "Ball," the Sun or Fire God. These priests offered up human sacrifices to their god for he was a "God" who rejoiced in the sacrifice of human victims and the tears of the victim's loved ones.

Since the time of the Carthagians, Malta has had many rulers—Romans, Arabs, Normans, Aragonese, Castillians, the Hospitalers or the order of St. John of Jerusalem, who were later known as the Knights of Rhodes, and still later as the Knights of Malta. After this France ruled the island for a short time before it became the British possession it now is.

However with all this varied history and regardless of the many nations who ruled them, the people of those islands still speak the ancient Caananite, Semitic tongue, the speech of the Phoecians. The mother tongue of Queen Dido, who was the founder of Carthage, for Malta was the birthplace of Carthage's most famous citizen—the man who made Rome tremble at the height of her power—Hannibal, one of the world's greatest generals.

On the northeast shore of Malta there are a number of large bays. One of these is known as Grand Harbour. This bay has a point of land extending into it upon which the capitol of the Maltese Islands—the city of Valletta—is built. A few miles inland from this town, toward the south, overlooking the plain which leads to the shore is a large plateau known as the Corradino. The little village of Casal Paula, with which we are interested, is built on this plateau and from the village one can view the capitol town of Valletta, Grand Harbour, the plain leading to it, and also look out to the sea.

In this small village of Casal Paula during the year 1902,

workmen who were digging a well literally fell into the Earth. They had once again uncovered the outer room of the Maltese Cave entrance. Since the well was to be dug for a house which was on the main street in Casal Paula (a street known as "Hal Saflieni") and because this first cave was later discovered to be a complex of caves, three of which were a series of chambers excavated out of solid rock on three even lower levels for each chamber. This entrance is known as the "Hypogeum of Hal Saflienti." A hypogeum is the Latin name for an underground structure.

Later this series of underground rooms were discovered to have been located in the middle of an ancient neolithic village. From the construction of the entrance stones, it is now assumed that at certain times a human sacrifice was chained before the entrance. The entrance and the walls of the ceilings of some of the passageways and rooms, have been found to be decorated with red ochre primitive art designs, but when first discovered, the three caves were crammed with as many as 30,000 skeletons of men, women and children. After all these bones were cleared out, the primitive murals were shown taking the form of diamond shapes as well as oblated and elongated ovals, all of which were joined together with wavy lines and whirls. These decorations had been created solely from the application of red ochre, which had been applied by the most primitive of methods.

Once past the entrance, a narrow passageway leads down into the first room. It is in this room that the "Oracle" may be found. The Oracle is a hemispherical hole in the wall; a hole which is lower than the mouth of an ordinary sized man. The hole is about two feet in diameter, and one can speak into it. A curved projection carved out of the back of the cave then acts as a sounding board. The voice is amplified and it resounds throughout all the other caves. It creates an effect which must have frightened the primitives into sacrificing many of the members of their tribe to the being who spoke with the "Voice of A God."

If you continue down through narrow and low passageways, you come to another room. The center of this room has a circular stone altar with tunnels in it, the use of which can only be guessed at. Carved in the walls of this room are many niches, the base of which are like bunk beds. They have hollows scooped out for the head and body as well as the feet of four-foot-high individuals,

26

while some are even smaller.

Leading from this room is a small, narrow passageway which leads downward, ending in another even larger underground room, a room which has narrow slit-like entrances into other small caves which surround it. One opening, however, is a window into another cave, the entrance of which is covered by a huge slab of stone. This window looks down into what was evidently a prison, but how any beings four feet tall were able to manipulate the huge stone slab must remain a mystery—perhaps for all time.

An opening in the wall opposite the entrance to this cave leads to a passage narrow and torturous, the entrance to the real caves. This passage ends on a pathway which extends along the side of a vast cleft in the Earth, a pathway which leads ever downward to the long underground tunnels and series of caves which are reputed to allow the venturesome one to traverse the entire length of the island and *even further.*

Legend has it that these passageways at one time connected with the underground crypts from which the Catacombs of Rome were created. This may very well be true, for the reader must remember that the Mediterranean Sea was created after neolithic times by huge earthquakes and the shifting of the Earth's crust. Therefore, while the ancient tunnels may have existed they might have been closed by cataclysms of this type, with only the knowledge of them coming down to us in legends which still persist.

There is an article written by Miss Lois Jessup, who is the secretary of the New York Saucer Information Bureau (better known as NYSIB) which appeared in an old issue of Riley Crabb's *Borderland Science* (and later reprinted in full in the book *Enigma Fantastique* by Dr. Allen). This article relates her trip to visit these caves, a visit which happened before the entrance of the caves leading from the third chamber were sealed off. Her story relates a view of weird type beings in these vast caverns. For plain suspense, it shouldn't be missed.

The tunnels under the "Hypogeum" have been sealed off ever since a school took 30 students into the caves and disappeared, guide and all. It was stated that the waves caved in on them. Strange to relate, however, search parties were never able to locate any trace of these people and children.

It has been asserted that for weeks the wailing and screaming of children was heard underground in different parts of the island, but no one could locate the source of the sound. If the walls caved in, why the cave-in could not be found and excavating to free those children, who were trapped underground, could not be undertaken, remain unanswered questions.

How the children could leave to scream for weeks later is another unanswered question. At any rate, the underground entrance to the caves in Malta has been sealed off, and no one is allowed to enter, *nor is anything allowed out!*

An Entrance to the Caves in Staffordshire, England

This entrance to the caves now lost, was discovered by a laborer, who was digging in a lonely field somewhere in Staffordshire, England. The exact location of the field and entrance has never been discovered. However, the story is related in *A History of Staffordshire*, by Dr. Plot, who wrote the book in the late 1770s.

I shall relate the highlights of the events as they appear in this ancient historical book.

A dull, ignorant laborer was digging a trench in a field which lay in a valley surrounded on almost all sides by woods somewhere in Staffordshire. The sun had gone down and the laborer, who later related his experience, asserted that just as he was about to stop work, his pick hit a large flat stone. The stone had an iron ring mounted in it. He stayed and cleared the stone, which was in the form of a large oblong.

His attempt to pry the stone up was met with failure, but he utilized ropes he had brought to obtain more leverage and managed to slide the stone over. This revealed a stone staircase, which sloped down into the Earth. Since his first thought was that this might lead to an ancient tomb containing treasure, he gradually descended the stone stairway. While looking back, he could still see the sky glowing with the last light of the sun. His descent continued until he was about, according to his estimation, 100 feet underground. It was at this point that he suddenly reached a sort of landing.

The planet Venus had risen by this time and was shining directly down the shaft, so that he was able to discern the beginning of another stairway, which descended at a right angle to the first one. The possibility of a treasure in gold or jewels, made him feel his way in the darkness down another 120 steps. At the foot of these steps was a turn, and far below down another long flight of stone steps, he could see a pale but steady light.

While descending this long flight of steps, he heard the sound of some sort of machinery or the rumble of a large vehicle somewhere far in the distance. He paused, frightened, but the sound was gone and in the surrounding stillness, he forced himself to go forward toward a light which glowed unnaturally in the bowels of the Earth.

Reaching the end of the steps, he found himself in a large stone chamber, the roof of which seemed far above him and the walls of which he could not see even by the light of a globe, which glowed on the floor before him. Suddenly a hooded cowled figure appeared from some side passageway. This being pointed what he described as a baton-like object—or as we would understand it, a tube—at the light and destroyed it with a thunderclap, which echoed and reechoed through immeasurable subterranean passageways.

The frightened laborer could not remember how he got out of the tunnel or up the stone stairway, when he related his story. Any attempts to get him to visit the valley again were unsuccessful. Others who searched for the digging were unable to locate either because of the terrible wind and rainstorm which occurred that night. This ripped and washed the vegetation of the valley away, leaving only the bare earth with no trace of the trench, the stone or the staircase. Because of this, the Staffordshire entrance has never been located again.

• • •

[Editor's Note: Dr. Robinson died years ago after a long illness. Death also claimed Jack's charming wife, Mary, herself a seeker of mystical truths. Dominick Lucchesi and Gray Barker are also no longer with us. But others have also taken up the search for the truth about these suspected underground bases.]

The Dulce Base

The underground Alien base outside of Dulce, New Mexico, is perhaps the one most frequently referred to. Its existence is most widely known, including several UFO abductees who have apparently been taken there for examination and then either managed to escape or were freed just in the nick of time by friendly Alien forces.

According to UFO conspiracy buff and ex-Naval Intelligence Officer Milton Cooper, "In 1969 a confrontation broke out between the human scientists and the Aliens at the Dulce underground lab. The Aliens took many of our scientists hostage. Delta forces were sent into free them but were no match against the Alien weapons. Sixty-six of our people were killed during this action. As a result we withdrew from all joint projects (with the Greys) for at least two years. A reconciliation eventually took place and once again we began to interact. Today the alliance continues."

Several months ago, researcher Jason Bishop III prepared a special, confidential, report on Dulce, the material for which came from people who *know* the Dulce underground base *really* exists! "They are," says Bishop, "people who worked in the labs, abductees taken to the base, people who assisted in the construction, intelligence personnel (NSA, CIA, etc.), and UFO/Inner Earth researchers." This information, notes Bishop, "is meant for those who are seriously interested in the Dulce base. For *your own protection,* be advised to '*use caution*' while investigating this complex." Though Bishop's investigation is ongoing, his preliminary findings are as follows:

Genetic Lab

The Dulce base is a "*genetics lab*" that is connected to Los Alamos, via a tube-shuttle. Part of the Grey's research is related to the genetic effects of radiation (mutations and human genetics). Its research also includes other "Intelligent Species" (Alien biological life form "entities").

In the revised September, 1950 edition of *The Effects of Atomic Weapons,* prepared for and in cooperation with The U.S. Department of Defense and The U.S. Atomic Energy Commission, under the direction of The Los Alamos Scientific Laboratory, we read about how "complete underground placement of bases is desirable." On page 381: "There are apparently no fundamental difficulties in construction and operating Underground various types of important facilities. Such facilities may be placed in a suitable existing mine or a site may be excavated for the purpose."

Caught in the Game

Centuries ago, surface people (some say The Illuminati) entered into a pact with an "Alien nation" hidden within the Earth. The U.S. Government, in 1933, agreed to trade animals and humans in exchange for high-tech knowledge, and to allow them to use (undisturbed) *underground bases,* in the Western U.S.A. A special group was formed to deal with the Alien beings. In the 1940's, "Alien Life Forms" (ALF) began shifting their focus of operations, from Central and South America, to the U.S.A.

The Continental Divide is vital to these "entities." Part of this has to do with magnetics (substrata rock) and high energy states (plasma). [See: *Beyond the Four Dimensions* (Reconciling Physics, Parapsychology and UFOs) by Karl Brunstein. Also: *Nuclear Evolution* (Discovery of the Rainbow Body) by Christopher Hills.]

*This area has a very high concentration of lightning activity; Underground waterways and cavern systems; fields of atmospheric ions; etc.

Whose Planet is This?

*These Aliens consider themselves "Native Terrans."

They are an ancient race (descended from a reptilian humanoid species which cross-bred with sapient humans). They are untrustworthy manipulator Mercenary Agents for another extraterrestrial culture (the DRACO) who are returning to Earth (their ancient "Outpost") to use it as a staging area.

But, these Alien Cultures are in conflict over whose agenda will be followed for this planet. All the while Mental Control is being used to keep humans "in place," especially since the forties.

The Dulce complex is a joint U.S. Government Alien Base. It was *not* the first built with the Aliens (others are in Colorado, Nevada, Arizona, etc.)

The Secret Activity

Paul Bennewitz reports about his study into the Dulce area: "Troops went in and out of there every summer, starting in '47. The natives do recall that. They also built a road—right in front of the people of Dulce and trucks went in and out for a long period.

"That road was later blocked and destroyed....The signs on the trucks were 'Smith' Corporation out of Paragosa Springs, Colorado. No such Corporation exists now—no record exists....I believe the base—at least the first one was being built then uncovering of a lumbering project...problem—they *NEVER* hauled logs. Only *BIG* equipment."

R & D and the Military Industrial Complex

The Rand Corporation became involved and did a study for the base. Most of the lakes near Dulce were made via government grants "for" the Indians.

Navajo Dam is the main source for conventional electric power, with a second source in El Vado (also an entrance).

"Note: If Rand is the mother of Think Tanks, then the Ford Foundation must be considered the father.

Rand secrecy is not confined to reports, but on occasion extends to conferences and meetings. On page number 645 of The Project Rand Proceedings of the *Deep Underground Construction Symposium* (March 1959) we read: "Just as airplanes, ships and automobiles have given man mastery of the surface of the Earth, tunnel-boring machines...will give him access to the Subterranean World."

Note: The September, 1983 issue of *Omni* (page 80) has a color drawing of "The Subterrene," the Los Alamos nuclear-powered tunnel machine that burrows through the rock, deep underground, by heating whatever stone it encounters into molten rock (magma), which cools after the Subterrene has moved on. The result is a tunnel with a smooth, glazing lining. These underground tubes are used by electromagnetically powered "Subshuttle Vehicles," which can travel at great speeds. They connect the "Hidden

Empire" Sub-City complexes. Also, the top-secret project code-named "Noah's Ark," uses "Tube-shuttles" in connection with a system of over 100 "Bunkers" and "Bold Holes" which have been established at various places on Earth, with other Bases inside the Moon and Mars. Many of these underground cities are complete with streets, sidewalks, lakes, small electric cars, apartments, offices and shopping malls.

There were over 650 attendees to the 1959 Rand Symposium. Most were representatives of the Corporate-Industrial State, like: The General Electric Company; AT&T; Hughes Aircraft; Northrop Corporation; Sandia Corporation; Stanford Research Institute; Walsh Construction Company; The Bechtel Corporation; Colorado School of Mines, etc.

Bechtel (pronounced BECK-tul) is a supersecret international corporate octopus, founded in 1898. Some say the firm is really a "Shadow Government"—a working arm of the CIA. It is the largest Construction and Engineering outfit in the U.S.A. and the World (and some say, beyond).

The most important posts in U.S.A. Government are held by former Bechtel Officers. They are part of "The Web" (an interconnected control system) which links the Tri-Lateralist plans, the C.F.R., the Orders of "Illuminism" (Cult of the All-seeing Eye) and other interlocking groups.

"The Monitors": Abductions

In the fifties, the EBES ("Greys") began taking large numbers of humans for experiments. By the Sixties, the rate was speeded up and they began getting careless (they didn't care). By the Seventies, their true colors were very obvious, but the "Special Group" of the Government still kept covering up for them. By the Eighties, the Government realized there was no defense against the "Greys." So...programs were enacted to prepare the Public for open contact with non-human "Alien" Beings.

The "Greys" and the "Reptoids" are in league with each other. But their relationship is in a state of tension.

The "Greys" only known enemy is the Reptilian Race, and they are on their way to Earth (inside a Planetoid).

Some forces in the Government want the public to be aware of what is happening. Other forces (The Collaborators) want to con-

33

tinue making "whatever deals necessary" for an elite few to survive the conflicts.

The Future could bring a Fascist "World Order" or a transformation of human consciousness (awareness). The struggle is NOW...your active assistance is needed. Prepare! We must preserve Humanity on Earth.

Mind Manipulation Experiments

The Dulce Base has studied mind control implants; Bio-Psi Units; ELF Devices capable of Mood, Sleep and Heartbeat control, etc.

D.A.R.P.A. (Defense Advanced Research Projects Agency) is using these technologies to manipulate people. They establish "The Projects," set priorities, coordinate efforts and guide the many participants in these undertakings. Related Projects are studied at Sandia Base by "The Jason Group" (of 55 Scientists). They have secretly harnessed the Dark Side of Technology and hidden the beneficial technology from the public.

Other Projects take place at "Area 51" in Nevada..."Dreamland" (Data Repository Establishment and Maintenance Land); Elmint (Electromagnetic Intelligence); Cold Empire; Code EVA; Program HIS (Hybrid Intelligence System): BW/CW; IRIS (Infrared Intruder Systems); BI-PASS; REP-TILES, etc.

The studies on Level Four at Dulce include Human Aura research, as well as all aspects of Dream, Hypnosis, Telepathy, etc. They know how to manipulate the Bioplasmic Body (of Man). They can lower your heartbeat with Deep Sleeve "Delta Waves," induce a static shock, then reprogram, Via a Brain-Computer link. They can introduce data and programmed reactions into your Mind (Information impregnation—the "Dream Library").

We are entering an era of Technologicalization of Psychic Powers.

The development of techniques to enhance man/machine communications; Nano-tech; Bio-tech micro-machines; PSI-War; E.D.O.M. (Electronic Dissolution of Memory); R.H.I.C. (Radio-Hypnotic Intra-Cerebral Control); and various forms of behavior control (via chemical agents, ultrasonics, optical and other EM radiations). The Physics of "Consciousness."

Better Living Through Bio-Tech?

The development of "Bio-Technologies" will mean a revolutionary change in the Life of every Human Being now on Earth!

Surviving The Future

The Dulce Facility consists of a central "Hub," the Security Section (also some photo labs). The deeper you go, the stronger the Security. This is a multi-leveled complex. There are over 3000 cameras at various high-security locations (exits and labs).

There are over 100 Secret Exits near and around Dulce. Many around Archuleta Mesa, others to the source around Dulce Lake and even as far east as Lindrich.

Deep sections of the Complex connect into natural Cavern Systems.

A person who worked at the Base, who had an "Ultra 7" Clearance, reports: "There may be more than seven Levels, but I only know of seven. Most of the Aliens are on 5-6-7 Levels. Alien housing is Level Five."

21st Century Power: "Bio-Tech"

We are leaving the Era of expendable resources, like Oil-based products. The Power of the Future is Renewable resources... "Biologically" Engineered. The Dulce Genetic Research was originally funded under the clock of "Black Budget" Secrecy (Billions $ $ $).

They were interested in intelligent "Disposable Biology" (humanoids), to do dangerous Atomic (Plutonium) Rocket and Saucer experiments.

We Cloned "our" own little Humanoids, via a process perfected in the Biogenetic Research Center of the World, Los Alamos! Now, we have our own disposable slave-race. Like the Alien "Greys" (EBES), the U.S. Government clandestinely impregnated females, then removed the Hybrid fetus (after about three months) and then accelerated their growth in the Lab. Biogenetic (DNA Manipulation) programming is instilled—they are "Implanted" and controlled at a distance through regular RF (Radio Frequency) transmissions. Many humans are also being "Implanted" with Brain Transceivers. These act as telepathic "Channels" and telemetric brain manipulation devices. The network-net was set up by DARPA (Advanced Research Project Agency). Two of the procedures were

35

R.H.I.C. (Radio-Hypnotic Intracerebral Control) and E.D.O.M. (Electronic Dissolution of Memory). The brain transceiver is inserted into the head through the nose. These devices are used in the Soviet Union and the United States, as well as Sweden. The Swedish Prime Minister Palme gave the National Swedish Police Board the right (in 1973) to insert brain transmitters into the heads of human beings COVERTLY!

They also developed ELF and E.M. wave propagation equipment (RAYS), which affects the nerves and can cause nausea, fatigue, irritability, even death. This is essentially the same as Richard Shaver's Cavern "Telaug" Mech. This research into biodynamic relationships within organisms ("BIOLOGICAL PLASMA") has produced a RAY which can change the "genetic structure" and "heal." Shaver's Cavern "BEN-Mech" could heal!

Warning: Manipulation and Control

FEAR, FRAUD AND FAVOR....The Pentagon, the CIA, NSA, DEA, FBI, NSC, etc. seek to capitalize on the beliefs of the American public. The Secret Government is getting ready to "stage" a contact-landing with Aliens in the near future. This way they can control the release of Alien-related propaganda. We will be told of an interstellar conflict.

But...what looks real, may be fake. What is disinformation? Is your attention being diverted by the strategy of a "shadow plan"?

Inside the Dulce Base

Security officers wear jumpsuits, with the Dulce symbol on the front, upper left side. The standard hand weapon at Dulce is a "flash gun," which is good against humans and Aliens. The ID card (used in card slots, for the doors and elevators) has the Dulce symbol above the ID photo. "Government honchos" use cards with the Great Seal of the U.S. on it. "The Cult of the All-Seeing Eye" (The *New World Order*) 13. "666" The Phoenix Empire..."9" "ILLUMINSIM"..."One out of many."

After the Second Level, everyone is weighed, in the nude, then given a uniform. "Visitors" are given an off-white uniform. In front of *all* sensitive areas are scales built under the doorway, by the door control. The person's card must match with the weight and code or the door wont' open. Any discrepancy in weight (any change over

36

three pounds) will summon Security. No one is allowed to carry anything into or out of sensitive areas. All supplies are put through a security conveyor system. The Alien Symbol language appears a lot at the facility.

During the construction of the facility (which was done in stages, over many years) the Aliens assisted in the design and construction materials. Many of the things assembled by the workers were of a technology they could not understand, yet...it would function when fully put together. Example: The elevators have no cables. They are controlled magnetically. The magnetic system is inside the walls.

There are no conventional electrical controls. All is controlled by advanced magnetics. That includes a magnetically-induced (phosphorescent) illumination system. There are no regular light bulbs. All exists are magnetically controlled. Note: It has been reported that, "If you place a large magnet on an entrance, it will affect an immediate interruption. They have to come and reset the system."

The Town of Dulce

The area around Dulce has had a high number of reported Animal Mutilations. The Government and the Aliens used the animals for environmental tests, psychological warfare on people, etc. The Aliens also wanted large amounts of blood for genetic, nutritional and other reasons.

In the book, *ET and UFOs—They Need Us, We Don't Need Them* by Virgil "Posty" Armstrong, he reports how his friends (Bob and Sharon) stopped for the night in Dulce and went out to dinner. "They overheard some local residents openly and vociferously discussing Extraterrestrial Abduction of townspeople for purposes of experimentation." The ET's were taking unwilling human guinea pigs from the general populace of Dulce and implanting devices in their heads and bodies. The townspeople were frightened and angry but didn't feel that they had any recourse, since the ETs had our government's knowledge and approval.

Recently, participants in a "field investigation" of the area near Archuletta Mesa, were confronted by two small hovering spheres. They all became suddenly ill and had to leave the area.

We have passed the point of no return in our interaction with the Alien beings. We are guaranteed a crisis which will persist until the final REVELATION (or conflict).

The crisis is here, global and real. We must mitigate or transform the nature of the disasters to come and come they will. Knowing is half the battle. Read the book, *The Cosmic Conspiracy* by Stan Deyo.

The Phantom Board: Above the Law

Most meetings of "The Dulce Board" are held in Denver and Taos (New Mexico). A former U.S. Senator has full knowledge of Dulce. He was among a group that included a number of very prominent government figures who toured the base. In 1979, an "animal mutilation" conference took place in Albuquerque, New Mexico. This meeting was used to locate researchers and determine what they had learned about the link between the "mute" operations and the Alien government.

Another Senator knows about the "Ultra" secrets at "Dreamland" and Dulce. Several of my official sources have confirmed this to me. So do many others in the government... this is what the UFO researchers are up against...so be careful. You now know more than they want you to know.

They also have underwater bases off the coast of Florida and Peru.

More detailed information will be released in the near future: photos, video tapes, documents, etc. Watch out for "Special Agents" among you now.

In the 1930s, *Division Five* of the FBI knew about the "Aliens."

A Fascist cabal within this country had John Kennedy assassinated. Look to the links within the larger Umbrella...the "WEB" of a fascist totalitarian secret police state...within the Pentagon; JCS; DIA, FBI (Division Five); DISC/DIS and the DIA. Note: The Defense Investigative Services insignia is a composite of the Sun's rays, a rose and a dagger, symbolizing "The Search for Information, Trustworthiness and Danger."

This links with caves used for "Initiation Rites" all over the world...ancient vaults, retreats, alien bases and inner-Earth civilizations.

Overt and Covert Research

As U.S. Energy Secretary, John Herrington named the Lawrence Berkeley Laboratory and New Mexico's Los Alamos National Laboratory to house new advanced genetic research centers as part of a project to decipher the Human Genome. The Genome holds the genetically coded instructions that guide the transformation of a single cell—a fertilized egg—into a Biological Being. "The Human Genome Project may well have the greatest direct impact on humanity of any scientific initiative before us today," said David Shirley, Director of the Berkeley Laboratory.

Covertly, this research has been going on for years at Dulce labs.

Level #6 is privately called "Nightmare Hall." It holds the Genetic Labs. Reports from workers who have seen bizarre experimentation are as follows: "I have seen multi-legged 'humans' that look like half-human/half-octopus. Also Reptilian-humans, and furry creatures that have hands like humans and cries like a baby, they mimic human words...also huge mixtures of Lizard-humans in cages." There are fish, seals, birds and mice that can barely be considered those species. There are several cages (and vats) of winged-humanoids, grotesque Bat-like creatures...but 3½ to seven feet tall. Gargoyle-like beings and Draco-Reptoids.

Level #7 is worse, row after row of thousands of humans and human-mixtures in cold storage. Here too are embryo storage vats of Humanoids, in various stages of development.

"I frequently encountered humans in cages, usually dazed or drugged, but sometimes they cried and begged for help. We were told they were helplessly insane, and involved in high-risk drug tests to cure insanity. We were told to never try to speak to them at all. At the beginning we believed the story. Finally, in 1978, a small group of workers discovered the truth. It began the Dulce Wars" (and a secret resistance unit was formed). Note: There are over 18,000 Aliens at the Dulce base.

In late 1979, there was a confrontation over weapons. A lot of scientists and military personnel were KILLED. The base was closed for a while....But, it IS currently active. Note: Human and animal abductions (for their blood and other parts) slowed in the mid-1980s, when the Livermore Berkeley Labs began production of artificial blood for Dulce.

William Cooper states: "A clash occurred wherein 66 people,

of our people, from the National Recon Group, the DELTA group, which is responsible for security of all Alien-connected projects, were killed."

The DELTA Group (within the Intelligence Support Activity) have been seen with badges which have a black Triangle on a red background.

DELTA is the fourth letter of the Greek alphabet. It has the form of a triangle, and figures prominently in certain Masonic signs.

Each base has its own symbol. The Dulce base symbol is a triangle with the Greek letter "Tau" (T) within it and then the symbol is inverted, so the triangle points down.

The Insignia of "a triangle and three lateral lines" has been seen on "Saucer(transport)Craft," The Tri-Lateral Symbol.

Other symbols mark landing sites and Alien craft.

Christa Tilton of Tulsa, Oklahoma experienced a terrifying abduction at the hands of aliens who took her to their underground base in Dulce, New Mexico.

Going Underground

Those that inhabit the interior of the Earth—regardless of their origins—offer both fascination and a high degree of danger to surface dwellers. To be taken to what is often a cold, dark place for either experimentation or interrogation can often prove to be a very nerve-wracking experience that is likely to put even the most sane and sober person "over the edge."

One individual who has managed to take her "adventures" and make something out of them is the charming Christa Tilton, who is editor and publisher of *Crux* (Box 906237, Tulsa, OK), a small magazine devoted to UFOs, abductions, underground bases, Cryptozoology, Fortean topics, as well as the gamut of the unusual. Christa has been quoted in many stories as she is the one who remains the most vocal about her experiences "underground," having been to the lower levels of the Dulce UFO base in New Mexico. Her experiences are "hair raising," to say the least, but she refuses to remain silent about them. In fact, she has lectured from time to time about what happened to her—and what COULD happen to you! She has even come across others who have had pretty much the same things take place in their lives. Christa has gone ahead and made some startling comparisons in the following special, confidential, report!

• • •

Several months ago, I became aware of two different cases, one of May of 1973 in which a Judy Doraty of Texas had an unusual experience in which she may have been taken to an underground facility, also an abduction case investigated by APRO and Paul Bennewitz, in which in May of 1980, a Myrna Hansen of New Mexico had a similar experience in which she also was taken to some type of underground facility.

Since I am doing the investigation into my own underground experience, I found that to be of help to me or anyone else that might have experienced anything similar, I was going to have to make myself read their transcripts. For months I would procrastinate because, I suppose, subconsciously I did not really want to relive this experience I had by reading about another person's experiences. Now I am glad I did. I finally am going to reveal some of the many correlations of all three of our cases in hopes that others will come forward with more information.

My experience happened in July of 1987. I had about a three hour "missing time" in which later, under hypnosis, I relived the most unusual night of my life. As you can see from drawing number one, I did not go willingly to the craft. Two small aliens dragged me by the two arms on my back to the craft after they rendered me unconscious. The next thing I remember is waking up on a table inside some type of small craft. A guide greeted me and gave me something to drink. I now believe it was a stimulant of some kind because I was not sleepy after I drank the substance. I was taken out of the craft and when I looked around I noticed I was standing on top of a hill. It was dark, but I saw a faint light near a cavern. We walked up to this area and it is then that I saw a man, dressed in a red military-type jump suit (like a pilot would wear). My guide seemed to know this man as he greeted he, as we came closer. I also noticed he wore some type of patch and was carrying an automatic weapon. When we walked into the tunnel, I realized we were going right into the side of a large hill or mountain. There we were met with another guard in red and I then saw a computerized checkpoint with two cameras on each side. To my left was a large groove where a small transit vehicle carried you further inside. To my right it looked like a long hallway where there were many offices. We took the transit car and went for what seemed to be a very long time to another secured area. It was then that I was told to step onto some type of scale-like device that faced a computer screen. I saw lights flashing and numbers computing and then a card was issued with holes punched into it. I would later realize it was used as identification inside a computer. I asked my guide where we were going and why. He didn't say too much the whole time except that he was to show me some things that I need to know for future reference. He told me that we had just entered Level One of the "facility." I asked what kind of facility it was and he did not answer.

The story is so very long and detailed and I hope to write more about it so I will highlight some of the things I saw and then compare them to what Judy Doraty and Myrna Hansen saw. I was taken to a huge-looking elevator that had no door. It was like a very large dumbwaiter. It took us down to Level Two, where there were two guards in a different color of jump suit and I had to go through the same procedure as I did on Level One. This time I was taken down a large hall and saw many offices that had computers that lined the wall. As we walked by, I noticed the lighting was strange in that I could not see a source for it. Other people walked by and never once acted like I was a stranger. I felt I was in a huge office building where there are many employees with many offices and cubicles. I then saw an extremely large area which looked like a giant factory. There were small alien-type craft parked at the sides. Some were being worked on underneath and it was then that I saw my first grey-type alien. They seemed to be doing the menial jobs and never once did they look up as we passed. There were cameras posted everywhere.

Then we arrived at another elevator and went down to Level Five. It was then that I felt a sense of extreme fear and balked. My guide explained that as long as I was with him that I would not be harmed. So we got off and I saw guards posted there at the checkpoint.

This time they were not friendly and were issuing orders right and left. I noticed that two of the guards seemed to be arguing about something and they keep looking over at me. I wanted to find the closest exit out of this place, but I knew I had come too far for that. This time I was asked to change clothes. I was told to put on what looked to me like a hospital gown, only thank God it had a back to it! I did as I was told because I didn't want to cause any trouble. I stepped onto this scale-like device and suddenly the screen lighted up and I heard strange tones and frequencies that made my ears hurt.

What I really thought was strange is that these guards saluted the guide I was with, although he was not wearing any military clothes. He was dressed in a dark green jump suit, but it had no insignia that I know of. He told me to follow him down this corridor.

44

As I passed the guard station, I noticed the humming of those cameras as they watched my every move. I was taken down another hall and it was then that I smelled this horrid smell.

Contrary to Judy and Myrna's stories, I knew what I was smelling, or at least I thought I knew. It smelled like formaldehyde. Because of my medical background I felt probably more comfortable with this situation because I had gone through it so many times before. We came to a large room and I stopped to look inside.

I saw these huge tanks with computerized gauges hooked to them and a huge arm-like device that extended from the top of some tubing down into the tanks. The tanks were about four feet tall, so standing where I was I could not see inside them. I did notice a humming sound and it looked as if something was being stirred inside the tanks. I started to walk closer to the tanks and it was at that time that my guide grabbed my arm and pulled me roughly out into the hall. He told me that it wasn't necessary to see the contents of the tanks; that it would only complicate matters. So we went on down the hallway and then he guided my arm into a large laboratory. I was so amazed because I had worked in one before and I was seeing machines that I had never seen before.

It was then I turned and saw a small grey being with his back turned doing something at a counter. I heard the clinking of metal against metal. I had only heard this when I was preparing my surgical instruments for my doctor in surgery. Then my guide asked me to go and sit down on the table in the middle of the room. I told him that I wouldn't do it, and he said it would be so much easier if I would comply. He was not smiling and I was scared. I did not want to be left in this room with this grey alien!

About the time I was thinking this a human man entered. He was dressed like a doctor, with a white lab coat on and the same type of badge I was issued. My guide went to greet him and they shook hands. I began shaking and I was cold. The temperature seemed awfully cold. My guide smiled at me and told me he would be waiting outside and I would only be there for a few minutes.

I began to cry. I cry when I get scared. The grey alien looked at me and turned around to continue what he was doing. The doctor called for more assistance and it was then that one other grey alien came in. The next thing I knew I was very drowsy. I knew I was being examined internally and when I lifted my head, I saw this horrid grey alien glaring at me with his large black eyes. It was then I felt a stabbing pain. I screamed and then the human doctor stood next to me and rubbed something over my stomach. It was cold. The pain immediately subsided. I could not believe this was happening to me all over again. I begged for them to let me go, but they just kept on working very fast.

After they were finished, I was told to get up and go into this small room and change back into my other clothes. I noticed blood, as if I had started my period. But, as I continued to get dressed and when I came out, I saw my guide speaking to the doctor in the corner of the room. I just stood there...helpless. I felt more alone then than I ever had in my life. I felt like a guinea pig. After we left the laboratory I was silent. I was angry at him for allowing this to happen to me again. But he said it was necessary. Told me to forget.

I saw more aliens pass us in the hall. Again, it is as if I was a ghost. I asked my guide to please explain this place to me. He told me it was a very sensitive place and I would be brought back again in the next few years. I asked where I was and he told me I could not be told for my own safety. We then got into the small transit car and it took us to the other side. It was there that I saw the most disturbing things of all. Unlike the other two women who saw cows being mutilated, I saw what looked to me to be people of all different types standing up against the wall inside a clear casing-like chamber. I went close and it looked as if they were was figures. I could not understand what I was seeing. I also saw animals in cages. They were alive. This was more disturbing to me than seeing the humans in the chambers. I saw tubes extending from the humans and the animals. I saw what looked to be technicians working. They never turned around and smiled or acknowledged my presence. I thought this was very strange. They looked like mindless robots doing a boring job in some dark forbidding mountain facility. I realized this place was not just run by aliens, but by some form of the military also. Security was high. It became almost impossible to try to get to the next level. Again there was an argument with the guards. For some reason I felt they did not feel I belonged there. THEY WERE RIGHT! We were not allowed passage to Level Six. I asked what was down there and was told that he wanted me to see a certain file and some photographs. He said that many of the employees have their living quarters there and I was told this level containing certain experiments that had gone "bad," so to speak, and it would be upsetting and not comprehensible to me at this time.

It was then that he guided me to the elevator and we started our climb up to Level One. When we finally got out to the outside entrance it was still dark. So I knew I had not been gone too long. In fact I felt I was right near the craft, north of Tucson, where I had been initially taken. I was very wrong. I was taken to the same craft and this time I remember the feeling of leaving the area. The craft went straight up and it seemed like forever, but I then began to feel the descent. I was strapped into a seat all the time so I did not see out. I was taken down to the ground through some type of beam. I felt like I was floating. I saw my aunt's car in the distance down the hill. I walked to the car and drove many miles back to Tucson. I still was in my dirty night-shirt that I had worn when I was summoned to get in the car and immediately drove to the designated area. In the morning, my friend, Barbara Coventry, saw the huge scratches on my back and it was then I knew something very strange had happened to me the night before. But, I did not know what it was. My memory had been blocked.

Correlations of Judy Doraty and Myrna Hansen's Abductions

• All three of us were taken to some type of laboratory underground and examined.
• All three of us experienced the same type of smells in this place.
• Judy Doraty and I saw cameras.
• Myrna Hansen and I both experienced a dampness in the genital area after our exam.
• All three of us described the same type of tanks with something in them.
• Myrna Hansen and I felt that something inside the tanks was circulating or being stirred.
• All three of us felt like we were part of some type of experiment.
• Myrna Hansen and I felt we were taken on elevators.
• Myrna Hansen and I felt we were taken to a base of operations or a core of activity.
• Myrna Hansen and I both saw military wear with patches

worn on the shoulder.

• Myrna Hansen and I both went through tunnels and saw machinery.

• All three of us felt something was done to erase our memory of what we experienced.

• Myrna and Judy saw animal parts and cows being dissected.

• I saw animals in a lab and what looked to be bodies in the clear casings.

• Myrna Hansen and I both had abdominal scars which interested the aliens.

• Myrna Hansen and I both had something stuck into our left ear.

• Myrna Hansen and I both walked past huge rooms.

• Myrna Hansen and I were both asked to remove our clothes before examinations.

• Judy Doraty and I saw the same type of swivel chairs and built-in tables.

• Judy Doray and I both saw tubes with liquid going elsewhere.

Although all three of us found out some information, Judy found out some very startling things. The aliens told Judy that our soil is contaminated and soon the poison will be found in "human excretions." Speaking of the poisoning—they told Judy it will appear shortly and humans will be affected. It will show up in a laboratory and a sickness will break out and a large number of people will be affected. They saw this would be a warning and when it happens there will need to be a "cleansing process." Whatever is found will be isolated by doctors in a lab and there will be a cure. This sounds so very much like the AIDS epidemic that hit several years ago. Judy would have had no way of knowing about AIDS in 1973. Maybe this is a warning...maybe we should hear the aliens out.

In the Nevada Aerial Research Newsletter I sketched some containers that reminded me of incubators. I saw little beings lying inside them. After being regressed by Budd Hopkins in 1987 I was able to sketch the room with the many incubators in it. I saw a woman with black hair who urged me not to go close to the incubators. It was then that she introduced me to "another" hybrid child of mine who looked to be round three to four years old. I was told that there was a different donor for this child. I was told that I could name her and also told that I would be seeing her again. When I did, she looked to be around 16 years old. I called her "Lyrra" and she was told that she would never be able to adapt to Earth as it is now. The child had been raised around a non-violent surrounding and I was told that it would surely be her death if she were to stay with me.

I asked how a child of four years old in 1987 could grow and look as she does now. The alien-hybrid "MAIJAN" tried to explain that their medical and scientific advancements from the past few hundred years enabled them to genetically accelerate the process of growth in just a matter of a few months and years in our time. I asked how this could be done and he explained that there is a chemical that can be given to a fetus that stimulates the growth hormone, much like our Pituitary gland. He told me that in time, our scientists would be able to manipulate the gland by stimulating it with this certain chemical hormone. I asked if our Doctors are aware of this process already and he said yes. He told me it had already been performed on animals in laboratories successfully, but they have been unable to successfully triumph with this process with human beings. He said that the few that were used in our own government experiments soon died. They became deformed and very ill. That was all that was explained to me at that time.

"LYRRA"
Cross between two hybrid donors.

Tucson—July 1987

Christa had driven to the north side of the Catalina Mountains. She encountered a craft and was approached by its occupants. She resisted and was physically pulled across rocky ground, damaging the nightshirt she was wearing and leaving scratches on her back (a woman friend, staying with her in Tucson, would later photograph the scratches). Also, she had locked her car door, but the aliens opened it anyway. There is little recall at present about what occurred on the craft, except there was some discussion about "emotions," "hormones" and a "chemical imbalance in the brain"; plus something was done to her ears. The aliens revealed to her that her daughter, too, had been abducted (she would later come to her mother with a "dream" of such an event). Shortly after this Tucson abduction, it was revealed to Christa (and not by aliens) that U.S. *government agents* witnessed and photographed the incident!

Boulders

Bases in the United States

Over 50 bases are known to exist in the United States, the majority of them in the West, but they also exist in other parts of the country. Many are linked by an underground rail system. Some are in the hands of "friendly" space beings or sub-surface dwellers while others have long ago been "taken over" by the greys, the Deros, or other negative entities who operate against humankind.

This is a run down of some of the U.S. bases that we know about:

Mount Rainier

Mount Rainier in Washington State plays a most important part in the history of UFOs in the United States. It was here, on June 24, 1947, that a private pilot by the name of Kenneth Arnold caught a glimpse of something "strange" flickering in the mid-afternoon sunlight. Looking out the cockpit window he observed a formation of space ships zipping along far faster than any object man could possibly have created at this time shortly after the Second World War. To his trained eye, they looked like "saucers skipping over the surface of water." Thus the term "flying saucer," which remained popular for many years until UFO eventually became the name generally applied to anything unusual seen in the heavens.

Mount Rainier has a long history of "strange" activity. Even the Indians, who lived for many centuries in this region, had high spiritual regard for the mountain. They saw it as a "sacred place," and noted the movement of the Sky Gods above as they went about performing their religious ceremonies.

There is a very active UFO base beneath Mount Rainier, from which emerges many dramatic-looking craft of various shapes and sizes. There are also said to be underground "vaults" which house ancient records of a mysterious race linked to the Lemurians of the

Pacific region of the globe.

These vaults contain various "plates" on which are engraved the history of the underground peoples of this region. Researcher F.L. Boschke has done an extensive study of the many mysteries of Mount Rainier, which is amply presented in the book titled *The Unexplained:*

"It is understandable that when volcanoes are inactive, they are covered with snow and ice. Many volcanoes rise out of 'the eternal ice.' One of the tallest volcanoes in the world is Mount Rainier, in Washington, in the northwestern United States. This mountain, which lies south of the port of Seattle, is 14,000 feet high and naturally the top of it is covered with ice. However, there is something strange about this ice. If Jules Verne had known about Mount Rainier, he would have made it the place where the travelers entered the Earth in his science-fiction novel *Journey to the Center of the Earth*. In this mountain, volcanic forces struggle with the eternal ice, and the result is a phenomenon unique on this Earth.

"For hundreds of years people had heard that the ice cap of Mount Rainier concealed a secret, a maze of corridors and caves. But not until 1970 did scientists begin a systematic investigation. It was necessary for them to do so, for shortly before, seismographs had recorded violent earthquakes in the gigantic crater of Mount Rainier, and indications were that the heat in the cone was increasing. The danger was obvious. If the ice melted, some 4,000,000 cubic yards of water would flow down the slopes from each of the two craters at the top of Mount Rainier. The water would tear stones, rocks, pebbles, and mud from the mountainside, trigger landslides, fill up the valleys, melt glaciers, and in general threaten everyone who lived nearby.

"In August, 1970, an expedition climbed to the top of the easternmost of the two craters. When they arrived, instead of the crater they saw a round hole 1,000 feet wide and 500 feet deep, filled with snow and ice. In the white mass they found three large holes sloping downward from the inner wall of the crater. The holes sloped downward at an angle of between 35 and 40 degrees.

"The descent was difficult and dangerous. Deep in the crater there were corridors in the ice, some of them as much as 30 feet wide and almost 15 feet in height. The members of the expedition took the danger in stride and continued to descend. The adventure led them into a tangle of large and small corridors, some of which branched off and then met again at some other point. It was less like a maze than a system of tunnels. Some corridors led directly to the center of the crater; other dark passages led to dead ends. At a certain depth the explorers found a broad "highway" which sometimes widened into a hall and which followed the circumference of the crater wall. This "highway" alone was over a half-mile in length! For the most part, the floor of the passages was damp, muddy, and strewn with broken rock.

"The system of tunnels was filled with strange and threatening noises. Hot steam piped, gurgled, and hissed from hundreds of places in the ground, carving its way through mud and potholes and melting the ice on the walls and ceilings, which dripped continuously onto the ground. At other points there were streams of foul-smelling, poisonous gases. In many places the path was not only dark but shrouded with clouds of vapor which concealed everything from view. All the moisture the crater contained rained down into the depths. Apparently a pond or a lake is located somewhere deep inside this underworld.

"A warm draft was blowing even at the tunnel entrances, more than 13,000 feet high in the crater wall. The temperature was 4° C. But on top of everything else, it was hot inside the tunnel system! The steam in the corridors was as hot as 56° C, and at one point the temperature of the rocky floor was 86° C.

"Struggling against the heat, vapor, water, and gas, the geologists recorded, measured, and made charts of what they found. They marveled at the steep descents and at the cathedral-like grottoes which had been melted out of the ice. At one point, when the ice above them was 400 feet thick, they made two amazing discoveries. On the ground before them lay the remains of a bird which as a rule inhabits the coast 60 miles away, and above them in the icy ceiling of the corridor they found a red woolen glove!

"Mysterious discoveries ought to occur in an adventure, and this adventure had its share. Up above, at the edge of the crater, the explorers found the remains of another bird. Could a storm carry birds as high as the top of the crater? Perhaps, like the glove, it was brought there by some mountain-climber long ago. Or perhaps the bird and the glove once lay on top of the crater ice, until snow covered them and the heat of the crater melted the ice, allowing both objects to slowly sink into the depths, covered with new layers of snow and ice. This may well be the case. However, no one doubts that Mount Rainier still contains many secrets and that there may be other explanations for the presence of the glove and the bird."

Mount Lassen

Few even know of the existence of Mount Lassen in Tehama County, California, never mind the fact that it is a portal to a sizeable underground city, which includes a UFO base that has been taken over in the past by the greys, but is now back in the hands of the Ashtar Command, who are using the base to operate a vast command post from which they can launch their disc-shaped vehicles into the air at a moment's notice. Several individuals have apparently made it to the outermost fringes of this city, but only one or two that I know of have actually been to the base inside Mount Lassen. On warm summer evenings when the midnight sky is clear, I'm told that brilliant "orange fireballs" can often be seen streaming in and out of the peaks of Lassen as the saucers venture to and fro from the underground home port. The following report from Ralph B. Fields indicates that there is an entrance to a "strange world" at this point that deserves to be checked out further.

• • •

In beginning this narrative and the unexplainable events that befell my friend and myself, I offer no explanation, nor do I even profess to offer any reason. In fact, I have yet to find a clue that will, even in part, offer any explanation whatever. Yet as it did happen, there must be some rhyme or reason to the whole thing. It may be that someone can offer some helpful information to a problem that just should not exist in these times of enlightenment.

To begin with, if we had not been reading an article in a magazine telling us about the great value of guano (bat droppings in old caves) that have accumulated over a great number of years, we would have continued to wend our merry way through life without ever having a thing to worry about.

But having read the article and as we were at the time living near a small town called Manten in Tehama County, California, we thought that that would be a good country to explore for a possible find of this kind. After talking it over for some time and as we had plenty of time just then, we decided to take a little trip up the country just back of us. As we were almost at the foot of Mount Lassen, that seemed the best place to conduct our little prospecting tour.

So collecting a light camping outfit, together with a couple of pup tents to sleep in, we started out on what we expected to be a three- or four-day jaunt up the mountain.

I guess we covered about ten or twelve miles on the third day and it was fast approaching time to begin to look for a place to spend the night and the thought was not very amusing and it had turned a little colder and we were well over 7,000 feet above sea level.

We soon found a sheltered place beneath a large outcrop of rock and set about making a camp. As I was always the cook and Joe the chore boy, I began getting things ready to fix us some grub and Joe began digging around for some dead scrub bush to burn. I had things all ready and looked around for Joe and his firewood. But I could see no signs of him. I began calling to him and he soon came into sight from around the very rock where we were making our camp. And I knew he was laboring under some great excitement as his face was lit up like a Christmas tree.

He had found a cave. The entrance was on the other side of that very rock. He was all for exploration right away. But I argued that we had better wait till morning. But he argued that in the cave it was always night and we would have to use flashlights anyway, so what would be the difference? Well, we finally decided that we would give it at least a once-over after we had had a bite to eat.

It wasn't much to call a cave at first as it had a very small entrance, but back about 20 feet it widened out to about 10 feet wide and around eight feet high. And it did reach back a considerable distance as we would see at least 100 yards and it appeared to bend off to the left. The floor sloped slightly down.

We followed to the bend and again we could see a long way ahead and down.

At this point we became a little afraid as we were some way into the mountain. The idea of being inside so far seemed to make us a little afraid. But we reasoned that inasmuch as there were no branches or connecting caves we could not get lost and therefore had nothing to be afraid of. So we went on.

We found no sign of anything that we could imagine to be our much sought guano nor signs of any animals being inside the cave.

I don't know how far we went, but it must have been a mile or two, as we kept on walking and the cave never changed its contour or size. Noticing this I mentioned it to Joe. We stopped to examine closer by the light of our larger flashlights. And we discovered an amazing thing. The floor seemed to be worn smooth as though it had been used for a long time as a path or road. The walls and ceiling of the cave seemed to be cut like a tunnel. It was solid rock and we knew that no one would cut a tunnel there out of rock as there had been no sign of mining operations. And the rock in the walls and ceiling was run together like it had been melted. Or fused from a great heat.

While we were busy examining the cave in general, Joe swore he saw a light way down in the cave. We started down the cave once more and found a light. Or I should say the light found us as it was suddenly flashed into our faces. We stood there blinded by it for a minute until I flashed my light at its source and saw we were confronted by three men.

These men looked to be about 50 or a little younger. They were dressed in ordinary clothes such as is worn by most working men in that locality. Levi type pants and flannel shirts and wool coats. They wore no hats. But their shoes looked strange as their soles were so thick they gave the impression of being made of wood.

We just stood there for a minute or two and looked at them. We had no idea there was anybody within miles of us and there stood three men looking at us in a cave a mile or so in the depths of old Mount Lassen.

I was scared. We were unarmed. And we knew nothing about these men. One of them spoke to us. He asked us what we were looking for. I told him, but I could see he didn't believe it. We both tried to convince him, but he just smiled. We had a little argument with him, but fearing they might be some criminal gang in hiding, we came to the conclusion that we had better retreat. Turning to go we were confronted by two more of them.

I can't find any way to express the fear and utter helplessness I felt in finding our retreat cut off. I do remember having remarked to Joe, "Well, it looks like we are behind the well-known eight-ball." I sure didn't feel as jovial as I spoke either. One of the strangers told us, "I think maybe you had both better come with us."

We were in no position to argue, though we both would have liked to do a little of that right there, but we had no way of enforcing our arguments. Where could a hero gain any credit in a place like that? So we permitted the five to escort us deeper into the depths of old Lassen.

They had led us farther down and I guess we had gone a couple more miles when we came to the first thing that really amazed us.

We came to a place where the cavern widened out a little and we saw some kind of machine, if it can be called that. Though I had no chance to examine it closely at the time, I did later and it was a very strange contrivance. It had a very flat bottom, but the front was curved upward something like a toboggan. The bottom plate was about eight inches thick and it was the color of pure copper. But it was very hard tempered. Although I have had a lot of experience with metals and alloys, I had no opportunity to examine it closely enough to determine just what it was. I doubt very much if I could. It had a seat in the front directly behind a heavy dashboard affair and there was a dial shaped in a semi-circle with figures or markings on it. I had not the slightest idea what they stood for, but they were very simple to remember. If there was a motor, it was in the rear. All I could see was two horseshoe or magnet-shaped objects that faced each other with the round parts to the outside. When this thing was in operation, a brilliant green arc seemed to leap between the two and to continue to glow as long as it was in operation. The only sound it gave off was a hum or buzz that sounded like a battery charger in operation.

The seat in the front was very wide. The only method of operation was a black tear-shaped object which hung from the panel by a chain. One of these men sitting in the middle took this thing and touched the sharp end to the first figure on the left side of the dial.

When he touched the first figure, the contraption seemed to move almost out from under us. But it was the smoothest and quietest take-off I ever experienced. We seemed to float. Not the slightest sound or vibration. And after we had traveled for a minute he touched the next figure on the dial and our speed increased at an alarming rate. But when he had advanced the black object over past the center of the dial, our speed increased until I could hardly breathe. I can't begin to estimate the distance we had traveled or our speed, but it was terrific. The two horseshoe objects in the rear created a green light that somehow shone far ahead of us, lighting up the cavern for a long way. I soon noticed a black line running down the center of the cavern and our inner-mountain taxi seemed to follow that.

I don't know how long we continued our mad ride, but it was long enough for us to become used to the terrific speed and we had just about overcome our fear of some kind of a wreck when we were thrown into another spasm of fear.

Another machine of the same type was approaching us head on. I could see that our captors were very nervous, but our speed continued. As the other machine became closer our speed slowed down very fast and we came to a smooth stop about two feet from the front of the other machine.

Our machine had no sooner stopped than our captors leaped from the machine and started to dash away. A fine blue light leaped from the other machine in a fine pencil beam and its sweep caught them and they fell to the floor of the cavern and lay still.

The figures dismounted from the other machine and came close to us. Then I noticed they carried a strange object in their hands. It resembled a fountain pen flashlight with a large, round, bulb-like affair on the back end and a grip something like a German luger. They pointed them at us.

After seeing what had happened to our erstwhile captors I thought that our turn was next, whatever it was. But one spoke to us.

"Are you surface people?"

"I guess we are, as this is where we came from very recently."

"We did the horloks find you?"

"If you mean those guys there," I pointed to the five motionless figures, "back there a few hundred miles." I pointed toward the way we had come in our wild ride."

"You are very fortunate that we came this way," he told us. "You would have also become horloks and then we would have had to kill you also." That was the first time I had realized that the others were dead.

They put their strange weapons away and seemed friendly enough, so I ventured to ask them the who and why of everything we had run into. I told them of our search for guano and how we had encountered the five horloks, as he called them. And also asked him about the machines and their operation and could we get out again? He smiled and told us.

"I could not tell you too much as you would not understand. There are so many things to explain and you could not grasp enough of what I could myself tell you. The people on the surface are not ready to have the things that the ancients have left. Neither I nor any one in any of the caverns know why these things work, but we do know how to operate some of them. However, there are a great many evil people here who create many unpleasant things for both us and the surface people. They are safe because no one on the surface believes us or them. That is why I am telling you this. No one would believe that we exist. We would not care, but there are many things here that the outer world must not have until they are ready to receive them, as they would completely destroy themselves, so we must be sure that they do not find them. As for the machine, I don't know how it works. But I know some of the principles of it. It works simply by gravity. And it is capable of reverse. The bottom plate of it always is raised about four inches from the surface of the floor. That is why there is no friction and has such a smooth operation. This object suspended from this chain is pure carbon. It is the key to the entire operation. As I told you before, I cannot explain why it runs, but it does. We want you two to return to where you came and forget about us. We will show you how to operate the sled and we want you never again to enter the cave. If you do and you do not encounter the horloks, we will have to do something about you ourselves so it would not be advisable to try to return at all events. One thing I can tell you. We never could permit you to leave another time."

He explained to us the operation of the machine and in some way reversed its direction. So thanking them, we seated ourselves in the sled, as he had called it, and were soon on our way back.

Our return trip was really something we enjoyed, as I was sure not to advance the carbon far enough on the dial to give us such terrific speed, but we soon found ourselves where we started from. The sled slid to a smooth stop and we jumped out and started up the cave afoot.

We must have walked a long way coming in, for we thought

we never would come to the surface. But at last we did. And it was late afternoon when we emerged.

We lost no time in making our way down the mountain, and Joe tells me that he isn't even curious about what is in that cave.

But I am. What is the answer to the whole thing? I would like to know. We had been told just enough for me to believe that down there somewhere there were and are things that might baffle the greatest minds of this Earth. Sometimes I am tempted to go back into that cave if I could again find it, which I doubt, but, then I know the warning I heard in there might be too true, so I guess I had better be of the same mind as Joe. He says:

"What we don't know don't hurt us."

Death Valley

If you are ever drive in Death Valley, California, and the engine on your car sputters to a halt, hopefully you'll have a car phone with you and be able to dial AAA or at least a local service station for assistance before the sun goes down. Local Indian legends have long told of a strange tunnel that runs beneath the desert, but how many white men know of the folklore of the nearby native inhabitants? And even if you did, chances are you would dismiss the many stories as "tall tales" told by those who are superstitious.

Bill Cocoran and Jack Stewart were two old miners who roamed the area around Death Valley quite freely for many years. Unlike other overly paranoid prospectors, Cocoran and Stewart weren't afraid of claim jumpers. In fact, they welcomed the company of others and often befriended travelers who had also heard that there was gold "beneath the sands." One time they invited into their modest home three men who were experiencing trouble with their car. Unable to find the necessary parts to repair the vehicle, the strangers had to stay as the guests of Bill and Jack for a couple of days, during which time they revealed an amazing story, as originally published in a book titled *Death Valley Men*.

• • •

...Thomason looked from Jack to Bill and asked, "How long have you men been in this country?"

Jack spoke before Bill had a chance. "Not very long," said Jack quietly. Bill glanced curiously at Jack but said nothing. If Jack thought that 30 years was not very long, that was all right with Bill.

Thomason said, "I've been in and out of the Death Valley country for 20 years. So has my partner. We know where there is lost treasure. We've known about it for several years, and we're the only men in the world who do know about it. We're going to let you two fellows in on it. You've been good to us. You're both fine fellows. You haven't asked us any questions about ourselves, and we like you. We think you can keep a secret, so we'll tell you ours."

Jack blew smoke and asked, "A lost mine?"

"No, not a mine," said Thomason. "A lost treasure house. A lost city of gold. It's bigger than any mine that ever was found, or ever will be."

"It's bigger than the United States Mint," said White, with his voice and body shaken with excitement. "It's a city thousands of years old and worth billions of dollars! Billions of Dollars! Billions! Not Millions. Billions!"

Thomason and White spoke rapidly and tensely, interrupting each other in eager speech.

Thomason said, "We've been trying to get the treasure out of this golden city for years. We had to have help, and we haven't been able to get it."

"Everybody tries to rob us," put in White. "They all want too big a share. I offered the whole city to the Smithsonian Institution for five million dollars—only a small part of what it's worth. They tried to rob us, too! They said they'd give me a million and a half, and not a cent more." White's fist crashed on the table. "A lousy million and a half for a discovery that's worth a billion dollars!" he sneered. "I had nothing more to do with them."

Jack got up and found his plug of tobacco. He threw away his cigarette and savagely bit off an enormous chew. He sat down and crossed his legs and glowered at White as he worked his chew into his jaw.

Bill's voice was meek as he asked, "And this place is in Death Valley?"

"Right in the Panamint Mountains!" said Thomason. "My partner found it by accident. He was prospecting down on the lower edge of the range near Wingate Pass. He was working in the bottom of an old abandoned shaft when the bottom of the shaft fell

62

out and landed him in a tunnel. We've explored the tunnel since. It's a natural tunnel like a big cave. It's over 20 miles long. It leads all through a great underground city; through the treasure vaults, the royal palace and the council chambers; and it connects to a series of beautiful galleries with stone arches in the east slope of the Panamint Mountains. Those arches are like great big windows in the side of the mountain and they look down on Death Valley. They're high above the valley now, but we believe that those entrances in the mountain side were used by the ancient people that built the city. They used to land their boats there."

"Boats!" demanded the astonished Bill, "boats in Death Valley?"

Jack choked and said, "Sure, boats. There used to be a lake in Death Valley. I hear the fishing was fine."

"You know about the lake," Thomason pointed his blue chin at Jack. "Your geology would tell you about the lake. It was a long time ago. Millions of years, probably. The ancient people who built the city in the caverns under the mountain lived on in their treasure houses long after the lake in the valley dried up. How long, we don't know. But the people we found in the caverns have been dead for thousands of years. Why! Those mummies alone are worth a million dollars!"

White, his eyes blazing, his body trembling, filled the little house with a vibrant voice on the edge of hysteria. "Gold!" he cried. "Gold spears! Gold shields! Gold statues! Jewelry! Thick gold bans on their arms! I found them! I fell into the underground city. There was an enormous room; big as this cañon. A hundred men were in it. Some were sitting around a polished table that was inlaid with gold and precious stones. Men stood around the walls of the room carrying shields and spears of solid gold. All the men—more than a hundred men—had on leather aprons, the finest kind of leather, soft and full of gold ornaments and jewels. They sat there and stood there with all that wealth around them. They are still there. They are all dead! And the gold, all that gold, and all those gems and jewels are all around them. All that gold and jewelry! Billions!" White's voice was ascending to a shriek when Thomason put a hand on his arm and White fell silent, his eyes darting about to the faces of those who sat around the table.

Thomason explained quietly, "These ancient people must have

been having a meeting of their rulers in the council chamber when they were all killed very suddenly. We haven't examined them very closely because it was the treasure that interested us, but the people all seem to be perfect mummies."

Bill squinted at White and asked, "Ain't it dark in this tunnel?"

"Black dark," said White, who had his voice under control again. His outburst had quieted him. "When I first went into that council room I had just some candles. I fumbled around. I didn't discover everything all at once like I've been telling you. I fell around over these men, and I was pretty near almost scared out of my head. But I got over that and everything was all right and I could see everything after I hit the lights."

"Lights? There were lights?" It was Bill asking.

"Oh, yes," said White. "These old people had a natural gas they used for lighting and cooking. I found it by accident. I was bumping around in the ark. Everything was hard and cold and I kept thinking I was seeing people and I was pretty scared. I stumbled over something on the floor and fell down. Before I could get up there was a little explosion and gas flames all around the room lighted up. What I fell over was the rock lever that turned on the gas, and my candle set the gas off. That was when I saw all the men, and the polished table, and the big statue. I thought I was dreaming. The statue was solid gold. Its face looked like the man sitting at the head of the table, only, of course, the statue's face was much bigger than the man's, because the statue was all in perfect size, only bigger. That statue was solid gold, and it is 89 feet, six inches tall!"

"Did you measure it," asked Jack, silkily, "or just guess at it?"

"I measured it. Now you'll get an idea how big that one room—that council room—is. That statue only takes up a small part of it!"

Steady and evenly, Jack asked, "Did you weigh the statue?"

"No," said White. "You couldn't weigh it."

Bill was puzzled. "Would you mind telling me how you measured it?" asked Bill.

"With a sextant," said White. "I always carry a sextant when I'm on the dessert. Then if I get lost, I can use my sextant on the sun or moon or stars to find myself on the map. I took a sextant angle of the height of the statue and figured its height out later."

"A sextant," said Bill, frowning heavily.

Jack said, "It's a part of a church, Bill. Never mind that....Tell us some more about this place. It's very interesting."

Fred Thomason said, "Tell them about the treasure rooms."

"I found them later." White polished his shining pate with a grimy handkerchief. "After I got the lights going I could see all the walls of this big room and I saw some doors cut in the solid rock of the walls. The doors are big slabs of rock hung on hinges you can't see. A big rock bar lets down across them. I tried to lift up the bars and couldn't move them. I fooled around trying to get the doors open. It must have been an hour before I took hold of a little latch like on the short end of the bar and the great big bar swung up. Those people knew about counter-weights and all those great big rock doors with their barlocks—they must weight hundreds of tons—are all balanced so you can move them with your little finger, if you find the right place."

Thomason again said, "Tell them about the treasure."

"It's gold bars and precious stones. The treasure rooms are inside these big rock doors. The gold is stacked in small bars piled against the walls like bricks. The jewels are in bins cut into the rock. There's so much gold and jewelry in that place that the people there had stone wheelbarrows to move the treasure around."

Jack sat up in sudden interest. "Wheelbarrows?" he asked, "wheelbarrows a million years old?"

"We don't know how old they are,' said Thomason, reasonably, "but the stone Wheelbarrows are there."

"Stone wheelbarrows," marveled Jack. "Those dead men must have been very powerful men. Only very strong men could push around a stone wheelbarrow loaded with gold bars. The wheelbarrows must have weighed a ton without a load in them."

"Yes," said Thomason, slowly, "the wheelbarrows are stone and of course they are very heavy—"

"But they're very easy to push around even with a load in them," White explained. "They're scientific wheelbarrows."

"No," objected Jack in a low tone of anguish.

'"Yes," insisted White, pleasantly sure of himself. "A small boy could fill one of those stone wheelbarrows full of gold bars and wheel it around. The wheelbarrows are balanced just like the doors. Instead of having the wheel out in front so that a man has to pick up all the weight with his back, these wise old people put the wheel almost in the middle and arranged the leverage of the shafts so that a child could put in a balanced load and wheel the barrow around."

Jack's heart was breaking. He left the table and threw his chew out the door. He went over to the stove with his cup. "Anybody want more coffee?" he asked. No one did.

Bill studied Thomason and White for several minutes. Then he asked, "How many times you been in this tunnel?"

"I've been in three times," said White. "That's counting the first time I fell in. Fred's been in twice; and my wife went part way in the last time we was in."

Mrs. White stroked her blond hair and said, "I thought my husband was romancing when he came home and told me what he found in the mountains. He always was a romancer. I was sure he was just romancing about this city he said he found. I didn't believe it until they took me into it. It is a little hard to believe, don't you think?"

Bill said, "It sure is." Jack stirred sugar into his coffee and sat down at the table again. Bill asked, "Did you ever bring anything out of the cave"?

"Twice," said Fred Thomason. "Both times we went in we filled our pockets with gems, and carried out a gold bar apiece. The first time we left the stuff with a friend of ours and and went to try and interest someone in what we'd found. We thought the scientists would be interested or the government. One government man said he'd like to see the stuff and we went back to our friend to get the gold and jewels and he told us he'd never seen them; and dared us to try to get them back. You see, he double crossed us. We were in a little trouble at the time and the loss of that stuff just put us in deeper. We couldn't get a stake because we were having hard work making anyone believe us. So we made another trip out here for more proof. That time we brought out more treasure and buried it close to the shaft entrance to the underground city before we went back to the Coast. I persuaded some university officials and some experts from the Southwest Museum to come out here with me. We got up on the Panamints and I could not find the shaft. A cloudburst had changed all the country around the shaft. We were out of luck again. The scientists became unreasonably angry with us. They've done everything they can to discredit us ever since."

Jack watched Thomason and White across the rim of his coffee cup. Bill said, "And now you can't get into your treasure tunnel. It's lost again That's sure too bad."

Thomason and White smiled. "We can get in all right," said Thomason in a genial voice his cold eyes did not support. Mrs. White smiled confidently and her husband bobbed his head. Thomason went on: "You've forgotten about the old boat landings on the Death Valley side of the Panamint Mountains. All we have to do is climb the mountain to the openings where the galleries come out of the city on the old lake shore. Do you know the mountains along the west side of Death Valley?"

"I been down there," said Bill.

Thomason turned to White: "How high do you think those galleries are above the bottom of Death Valley?

White said, "Somewhere around forty-five hundred or five thousand feet. You looked out of them; what do you think?"

"That's about right," agreed Thomason. "The openings are right across from Furnace Creek Ranch. We could see the green of the ranch right below us and Furnace Creek Wash across the valley. We'll find those windows in the mountains, all right."

"You goin down there now?" asked Bill.

"That's what we came for," said Thomason. "We're going to take out enough gold to finance ourselves, and we'll open that city as a curiosity of the world."

"That's it," said White. "We're through with the scientists. We tried to make a present of our discovery to science because we thought they would be interested. But they tried to rob us, and then laughed at us and abused us..."

Saying thanks and farewell the treasure hunters left, promising to return, and drove in their car down Emigrant Canyon towards Death Valley. Later that same afternoon Bourke Lee met the three of them on the floor of the valley. Their car was parked beside the road between Furnace Creek Ranch and the Salt Bed. The men were patching a tube. They did not need any help, so he said goodbye and went south in the valley. He never saw Fred Thomason, Mr. White or his wife again, and ten days later when he again visited Bill Corcoran and Jack Stewart they told him that they hadn't seen them since.

When another week went by and the proprietors of the lost city

67

did not reappear, the author and Bill made a trip down into Death Valley in their car and took along a pair of field glasses, hoping to see some sign of the explorers or the "windows in the side of the mountain." They failed to find any sign of either.

• • •

Almost 20 years after this story was published, there appeared an article in the September, 1949, issue of *Fate* magazine, which tends to support the story of Thomason and White. The article was titled *Tribal Memories of the Flying Saucers,* written by a Navaho Indian, Oge-Make.

Most of you who read this are probably white men of a blood only a century or two out of Europe. You speak in your papers of the flying saucers or mystery ships as something new, and strangely typical of the twentieth century. How could you but think otherwise? Yet if you had red skin, and were of a blood which had been born and bred of the land for untold thousands of years, you would know this is not true. You would know that your ancestors living in these mountains and upon these prairies for numberless generations, had seen these ships before, and had passed down the story in the legends which are the unwritten history of your people. You do not believe? Well, after all, why should you? But knowing your scornful unbelief, the storytellers of my people have closed their lips in bitterness against the outward flow of this knowledge...

Let us say that it is dusk in that strange place which you, the white man, calls 'Death Valley.' I have passed tobacco (with us a sacred plant) to the aged chief of the Paiutes who sits across a tiny fire from me and sprinkles corn meal upon the flames. You sprinkle holy water, while we sprinkle corn meal and blow the smoke of the tobacco to the four directions in order to dispel bad luck and ask a blessing...

The old Paiute smoked my tobacco for a long time before he reverently blew the smoke to the four directions. Finally he spoke.

"You ask me if we heard of the great silver airships in the days before white man brought his wagon trains into the land?"

"Yes, grandfather, I come seeking knowledge." (Among all tribes of my people, grandfather is the term of greatest respect

68

which one man can pay to another.)

"We, of the Paiute Nation, have known of these ships for untold generations. We also believe that we know something of the people who fly them. They are called The Hav-musuvs."

"Who are the Hav-musuvs?"

"They are a people of the Panamints, and they are as ancient as Tomesha itself..."

"When the world was young, and this valley which is now dry, parched desert, was a lush, hidden harbor of a blue water-sea which stretched from half way up those mountains to the Gulf of California, it is said that the Hav-musuvs came here in huge rowing ships. They found great caverns in the Panamints, and in them they built one of their cities. At that time California was the island which the Indians of that state told the Spanish it was, and which they marked so on their maps.

"Living in their hidden city, the Hav-musuvs ruled the sea with their fast rowing-ships, trading with far-away peoples and bringing strange goods to the great quays said still to exist in the caverns.

"Then as untold centuries rolled past, the climate began to change. The water in the lake went down until there was no longer a way to the sea. First the way was broken only by the southern mountains, over the tops of which goods could be carried. But as time went by, the water continued to shrink, until the day came when only a dry crust was all that remained of the great blue lake. Then the desert came, and the Fire-God began to walk across Tomesha, The Flaming-Land.

"When the Hav-musuvs could no longer use their great rowing-ships, they began to think of other means to reach the world beyond. I suppose that is how it happened. We know that they began to use flying canoes. At first they were not large, these silvery ships with wings. They moved with a slight whirring sound, and a dipping movement, like an eagle."

The Chief continued by saying, "They are a beautiful people. their skin is a golden tint, and a head band holds back their long dark hair. They dress always in a white fine-spun garment which wraps around them and is draped upon one shoulder. Pale sandals are worn under their feet..."

• • •

I do not profess to know who is in "charge" of the tunnels beneath Death Valley at this time, though I suspect that they are still fairly active, as I do know of many passing through this region who have encountered UFOs on the highway late at night and experienced "missing time." Several of the abductees have personally told me that they were examined and that implants were surgically "put into place," while they were held "captive" somewhere underground in this area. None of those I have spoken with say that they have otherwise been hurt, but then again others might have been "taken" and we might never hear from them again, so I'd say travel here at your own risk.

Superstition Mountains

One place you should really stay as far away from as possible is Arizona's Superstition Mountains. True, there are all sorts of stories which maintain that vast tunnels containing millions of dollars in hidden treasure left by the Spanish and protected by the Indians, are available for the "lucky" treasure hunter, but so far there have been so many strange deaths—murders, actually—and disappearances in the Superstition Mountain range that you're better off alive and poor, rather than dead and potentially rich.

Researcher/publisher Timothy Green Beckley gives us a rather hair-raising rundown of some of the weird events which have taken place in the Superstitions over the course of many years.

• • •

As they continued their journey deeper into the cavern, the moaning continued to grow louder and louder and the air became heavy with a sulfuric odor. After they had descended about a thousand feet, they came to a side drift with its mouth almost closed from a fall of rocks.

A short distance down this drift they stumbled over a pile of bones which they estimated to be the skeletons of a dozen or more persons. Searching around, they soon discovered various bits of broken Indian pottery. In the drift they neither saw the flashes nor heard the moans, but the poisonous air made them quite drowsy. Because of this situation they soon found it impossible to continue any further and thus they had to return to the surface. It is not known to this day if this entrance has ever been relocated by anyone else.

Those who have dared brave the shadows of the Superstition Mountains say that there is something that puts evil in the minds of people who go into the mountains in search for the Lost Dutchman Mines!

Probably the richest treasure yet to be found by man is located somewhere within the bowels of the Earth in these mysterious mountains. In search for this treasure many people have been killed; many others have died of mysterious causes while still others have met death at the hands of fellow prospectors who crave one of the Earth's greatest treasures—GOLD!

Indeed just what is it that makes men go start raving mad upon the mountains that make up the great Superstition Range? Is it the blood thirsty lust for this precious metal or something far more sinister and perhaps supernatural?

Benjamine M. Ferrira of Honolulu, Hawaii, told staff reporter Jack Karie of the *Arizona Republic*, while serving a sentence in jail for the killing of his gold-seeking partner on April 19, 1959 that:

> "There is something that happens to the minds of people going into that Mountain to look for gold. People just get started hating each other—first thing you know they're at each other's throats.
>
> "It didn't make sense! There's something there on that mountain that makes men foolish. I know from experience—from a very sad experience—that mountain does things to the minds of men. At least I think I went completely nuts—one time I thought those canyon walls were moving in on me."

Some months later, in November, Laven Rowlee of Phoenix was shot to death by Ralph Thomas after a life and death struggle that took place just southeast of the famous Weaver's Needle, named for its discoverer Pauline Weaver. Mrs. Thomas asserted, according to a special report in the *Arizona Republic*, that Rowlee first approached the couple "jabbering something about us trying to kill him—he said my husband was an FBI agent. I really didn't understand what he was talking about. It sounded like a lot of

71

gibberish."

After Rowlee attacked the couple they somehow managed to grab his gun and overpower him. As the two proceeded to march Rowlee to a nearby prospector's camp, he screamed, "I've got another one." Thinking Rowlee meant a gun, Thomas fired and knocked Rowlee down with a shot from his own hand weapon. Rowlee died a few hours later.

But the stories coming out of this area, from those who have seen the vast mountain range and know its innermost secrets, often reveal strange circumstances which refuse to be put to rest. Many of them could well be the product of overworked imaginations caused by the hot desert sun and the fearful winds that howl through the mountain passes like the sound of those from another world beckoning to those that dare set foot on its sacred ground.

In May of 1959, two dingy, dirty, sweaty prospectors told a strange story while visiting with an old time resident of the Phoenix area. They claimed that for several days they noticed what they at first thought to be several small children playing near and in a small creek which had water in it only during the early spring season. To find children so far from any desert dwelling or residential area puzzled the two. They were quite familiar with the many "strange" deaths that had occurred in this area and wisely felt that children had no business there. These small "children" appeared to be about five or six years old and would be seen in the same dry creek bed day after day as the prospectors went about their diggings. One day they decided to investigate and see what children could possibly be doing in such an area. When they reached the creek bed they discovered, to their amazement, that the "children" had completely vanished but there, still very fresh in the sand, were footprints. These prints appeared as MINIATURE DUPLICATES OF ENGINEER BOOTS. Although the miners returned to the same spot the next day they reportedly never saw the "children" again.

Other witnesses claim to have seen these little "children" at closer range and say they look more like men than children. Some ranchers, while on roundups in this same area, say that they could clearly see "little men" as they called them, on the tops of ridges and mountains of the superstition range watching them. Not one of those present on the roundups would bother them but would only gaze silently at them as they went on about their work.

About 19 years ago, a teenage boy working with a large ranch concern on roundup was somehow lost from the rest of the crew and wandered about the area for several days without either water or food. This, as any prospector or treasure hunter worth his salt can tell you, is more often than not very fatal. He passed into a semi-conscious twilight between consciousness and unconsciousness.

During the time he was in this state he was aware of several little men around him giving him continued help and directions. They finally were able to lead him out of the range where he finally made it to Gobe, Arizona, a distance of about 50 miles from where he was lost. They did not give him either food or water, but somehow he had strength. He could plainly make the people out and thus he was not sure whether they were "ghosts" or real things. But he did manage to say a few words to them and they in turn to him.

Brian Scott's Experiences

At least four or five individuals have come forward to tell of their "wanderings" underground inside the Superstition UFO base. Two of these individuals I know of have lost their sanity, while the others have either had nervous breakdowns or have vanished from their hometowns in order to go into seclusion. Only one man, Brian Scott, has publicly aired his story, and the UFOnauts he encountered at this base turned out to be rather deadly, as his home became haunted, his bedding caught on fire, and some time later he became possessed by negative entities.

Before his encounter, Brian Scott had led a hardworking existence. It was while he was on vacation in March of 1971, not far from the famed Superstition Mountain range, that he was "beamed" onto a craft underground with a purplish light emanating from its underside. Inside the ship, he was taken to a "darkened compartment" where seven-foot-tall creatures "moved their hands over my body and disrobed me."

Scott described the UFOnauts as being "large—very bulky—but with two arms and two legs, like humans." In appearance, he admits they "gave me the willies," explaining that they had skin textures that were a cross between an elephant, rhinoceros, and crocodile." As for their faces, "ears would start at the top of their head and run all the way down the whole side of their face, and

73

they had an extra layer of what seemed to be hide which covered them from approximately just below the chest to just below the knees. They also had a bit of an odor about the breath, which reminded me of dirty socks."

Subsequently, Brian claims four additional encounters with the identical group of aliens, plus meeting a being who is almost totally human in appearance and who calls himself "the host." Placed in a hypnotic trance by Dr. Alvin Lawson of California State University (Long Branch) Scott revealed in amazing detail how his hands and feet were up against one of the walls of the ship, spread-eagled, and he found it impossible to move. "In front of me," recalls Scott, "was this box-shaped thing—a machine. One of the creatures standing next to me made a couple of gestures with his hand and the machine began moving up, starting from my feet, to the top of my head, as if photographing my insides."

Scared to the breaking point, Scott urinated in his pants. "I thought I was going to die right then and there. A terrific pain was building in my head, like 10,000 migraine headaches all clumped into one. I tried to fight, but was held in place by some mysterious force. There was this one really big guy who seemed particularly interested in me. He placed his hand on my forehead and it felt like we were exchanging thoughts."

Since the day of his encounter, Scott says his brain has been functioning much faster than usual. While he possessed no formal technical training (nor was he a college graduate) prior to his experience, today the Garden Grove, California resident is a highly paid draftsman, the ability having been "given" to him, he insists, by the creatures aboard the UFO.

Even more remarkable is the fact that Brian periodically falls into deep trances, during which time an entity that identifies itself solely as "Asta" speaks, giving technically advanced data not normally known to the contactee. Voice prints made by the Rohe Scientific Corporation and studied under the supervision of researchers from UCLA, indicate that the voice patterns "could not technically have been made by a human being," but resemble the patterns made by a machine, perhaps a robot or computer.

Bizarre lights have also invaded the Scott home on numerous occasions, and the police were called at least once when Brian disappeared inside the house and could not be found by his wife, though he was dressed only in boxer shorts. Hours later he was found wandering in a daze in the back yard, supposedly after being brought back to Earth by the UFOnauts.

Research was conducted at the time by such groups as the then-prestigious Aerial Phenomena Research Organization, and Brian is convinced that "the beings who contacted me are preparing for what might turn out to be a mass landing on Earth, not too long in the future."

Quite certainly something "big" is in the works! The UFO-nauts seem to be building upon a well-designed plan of operation that they apparently want us to know little about, until just the right moment.

Indications are this might be the year chosen for establishing some form of "open contact" with mankind, but the question is—can society handle the abrupt changes that most assuredly would come if we were to form a channel of communication with stellar beings?

Mt. Shasta

One of the UFO underground bases the "good guys" are definitely in control of, is the base beneath Mt. Shasta in northern California.

The tunnels under Mt. Shasta are vast and house equipment and ships you wouldn't believe could possibly exist. There are teleportation and levitation devices, huge (by our definition) "Mother-Ships," and a crystal almost the size of a New York City skyscraper.

From all over the globe, hundreds of New Agers visit this site annually, and some even make this their home. Quite a number of "space channels," are known to operate in the area, such as Sister Thedra, who has been channeling Ashtar as well as other Space Guardians, not to mention Count Saint Germain, who has been known to visit here in his physical body from time to time.

Mt. Shasta is rich in the lore of the occult and metaphysics. It is truly a spiritual focal point for this planet. Deep from beneath the ground—where only the most aware are allowed—a full-time operation is constantly being carried out to save the Earth.

I have been told by sources whom I trust completely that the base was originally established by the people of Lemuria, a great continent that once existed in the middle of the Pacific; but just like its sister continent Atlantis, was destroyed due to the greedy nature and negativity of a few foolish leaders who were bent on planetary—as well as interplanetary—conquest.

So many "odd and peculiar" happenings have transpired around and in Mount Shasta that it would take several volumes to even penetrate the surface of all this material. The Lemurians—some of whom still reside here—are often seen wandering in the region. They can be recognized due to the fact that they are quite tall—in the eight and nine foot range. They even have their own underground city here, and it's all made of gold. Even the nature spirits—the knomes, the elves and the fairies—run about here non-disturbed, and many "outsiders" will tell you that they've heard the sound of far away flutes, which are the favorite instrument of the elemental kingdom. The only "unusual dweller" around these parts I might be the least bit cautious of would be our hairy friend Bigfoot, who has been known to scare the living hell out of hikers who go away not being such "happy campers," mainly due to the somewhat non-appealing scent he has been known to toss off.

I've been told that Mt. Shasta has a highly charged aura which prevents the forces of darkness from penetrating anywhere nearby. Teams of Lemurians, Space Brothers and elementals working jointly, meditate daily underground here to heal the planet and to keep this sacred spot safe from either physical or mental attack. Those that have been in the tunnels underground are never the same, their whole life so changed by what they have seen and heard!

There is even one instance that I know of where a young woman—just recently married—was healed by the rays of a space ship that hovered over her small camp. Hanna Spitzer told her amazing story in an old issue of Tim Beckley's *UFO Review,* from which I have his permission to quote excerpts:

"My husband, Damian, and I came to Mt. Shasta just last September. We were drawn here by the majesty that surrounds this area. Damian had been here before and so he was familiar with the surrounding communities and the people who reside near this locale.

"Our closest friend, Patrick, a very talented young artist, had been my husband's companion on his earlier visit, and he also was captivated with Mt. Shasta. As luck had it, he was to be commissioned by a local restaurant owner to paint a huge mural of Mt. Shasta and the many legends that have long surrounded this magical mountain.

"Quickly, we moved up the side of the mountain and set up camp. From here we had a picturesque view of Mt. Shasta City. This tiny village consists of ski shops and sleepy little hide-a-ways, with a few occult bookstores and health food stores thrown in for good measures. At one of the stores, someone told us about a strange light that had been seen while this person was out camping on the same property where we were living. Apparently, she awoke from a deep sleep and saw numerous flashing lights and heard a whooping noise. When she went into town the next morning she found that others had undergone similar experiences.

"Throughout our stay, Patrick kept telling us about a wonderful lady, a very gifted psychic, who was said to be a real 'powerhouse,' and who could attract a lot of phenomenon herself. Her name was Aendreious, and Patrick had invited her to come and stay with all of us. I was really fascinated by what I had heard, and couldn't wait to meet this woman.

"One day when Damian was in town doing some chores a striking woman in a turban approached him. It was Aendreious. Damian brought her up to the land that afternoon and immediately we were struck by her presence. As gifts, she had brought each of us a crystal. She spoke in a very knowing manner. On top of this, she was very meditative and peaceful and extremely fascinated with the mountain. Through this lady we learned quite a lot about magnetism and attraction. I knew—as we all did—that if we were to have a sighting, it would be while she was living with us.

"Aendreious had a wonderful attitude about flying saucers and aliens. She thought of them as masters, not little green men to be afraid of. Her talking calmed me a bit and I soon lost any fear I might have had. For days the men had been teasing me about the dark and about creatures who would try to gab me and take me away.

"Going into town became an experience in itself. We loved to speak with the people there and hear about their experiences first hand. There was one charming lady who walked through the streets talking to everyone she met about the saucers. She always wore a shiny yellow hat and seemed very devoted to her task."

• • •

William F. Hamilton III—Bill to just about anyone who knows him—became fascinated with the mystery of Mt. Shasta after reading the book *A Dweller on Two Planets,* by Phylos. This as even before his first visit to the mountain which—believe it or not—took place when he was just 15 years old.

I would suppose it was sometime later, however, that Bill actually began to look into the rumors and stories regarding underground bases which are known to criss-cross this country—not to mention the rest of the world!

Then finally in 1977, the veteran researcher whose work is highly respected by other UFOlogists, had a first-hand encounter with a young woman who sent his mind whirling and his thoughts buzzing. For this attractive—but very exotic looking—lady revealed that she was not a full time inhabitant of our world, but was actually a resident of an underground city located at the very heart of Mt. Shasta. Extracts of what she revealed to Bill regarding her subterranean domain, and her people's origins, their ongoing contact with outer space beings, was all part of their conversation which took place during several meetings. The woman's story—as you will see in just a moment—is utterly fascinating and deserves the attention of anyone doing serious research into underground cities and bases.

• • •

The Girl From Beneath Mt. Shasta

I run across some fascinating people in the course of my investigations who tell me many unusual stories. While on the trail of reports of UFO base locations, I met a young, very pretty blonde girl with almond-shaped eyes and small perfect teeth, whose name was Bonnie. Bonnie has told me an incredible story and has related a volume of interesting information on Atlantis and Lemuria. Bonnie is sincere, cheerful, and rational, and says she is a Lemurian born under the sign of Leo in 1951 in a city called *Telos* that was built inside an artificial dome-shaped cavern in the Earth a mile or so beneath Mt. Shasta, California.

Bonnie, her mother, her father Ramu, her sister Judy, her cousins Lorae and Matox, live and move in our society, returning frequently to *Telos* for rest and recuperation.

Bonnie relates that her people use boring machines to bore tunnels in the Earth. These boring machines heat the rock to incandescence, then vitrify it, thus eliminating the need for beams and supports.

A tube transit train system is used to connect the few Atlantean/Lemurian cities that exist in various subterranean regions of our hemisphere. The tube trains are propelled by electromagnetic impulses up to speeds of 2500 mph. One tube connects with one of their cities in the Mato Grosso jungle of Brazil. The Lemurians have developed space travel and some flying saucers come from their subterranean bases. Bonnie says her people are members of a federation of planets.

They grow food hydroponically under full-spectrum lights with their gardens attended by automatons. The food and resources of Telos are distributed in plenty to the million-and-a-half population that thrives on a no-money economy. Bonnie talks about history, of the Uighers, Naga-Mayas, and Quetzels, of which she is a descendant. She recounts the destruction of Atlantis and Lemuria and of a war between the two superpowers fought with advanced weaponry. She says the Atlanteans built a huge crystal-powered beam weapon that was used to control a small moon of Earth as a missile to be aimed at China, but their plans went awry and the moon split in two, coming down into the Atlantic, north of Bermuda, deluging the remaining isle of Atlantis. She claims her people are now part of a much greater underground kingdom called Agharta—ruled by a super race she calls "Hyprobeans."

I met Bonnie's cousin, Matox, who, like her, is a strict vegetarian and holds the same attitudes concerning the motives of government. They constantly guard against discovery or intrusion. Their advanced awareness and technology helps them to remain vigilant. Will we openly meet these long-lost relatives of ours? Bonnie says yes, but this is part of her incredible mission. Her mission—to warn those who will listen of the coming cataclysms that will culminate at the end of the century in a shift of the Earth's axis. After this catastrophe, she says the world will be one, and the survivors will

79

build a new world free of worry, poverty, disease and exploitation. The world will exist on a higher plane of vibrations and man will come to know his true history and heritage.

Science fiction? Bonnie is a real person. Many have met her. Is she perpetrating a hoax? For what motive? She does not seek publicity and I have a devil of a time getting her to meetings to talk with others, but she has done so. There has been little variation in her story or her answers in the past three years. She has given me excellent technical insight on the construction of a crystal-powered generator that extracts ambient energy. She has given me new insights on UFOs and their purpose in coming here. Bonnie's father, the Ramu, is 300 years old and a member of the ruling council of Telos.

Many tunnels are unsafe and closed off. All tube transit tunnels are protected and are designed to eject uninvited guests. Does Bonnie have the answers that we are looking for? I don't know. I am not making the claims nor can I provide proof. Bonnie says she would like to satisfy our need for proof and will work with me on a satisfactory answer to that problem, but she is unconcerned with whether people accept her or not. Bonnie is humorous and easy-going and well-poised, yet sometimes she becomes brooding and mysterious. She says her people are busy planning survival centers for refugees. One of these is to be near Prescott, Arizona.

Following is a question and answer session between Mr. Hamilton and Bonnie, which was done to answer even more questions about this underground world we are so intrigued by:

Q. Were there ten races on Lemuria?

A. They were called sub-races. There was only one race.

Q. Can you date that?

A. That was approximately 200,000 years ago.

Q. You once said that the early Lemurians come from the planet Aurora?

A. Yes, and at that time the sun (of Earth) was giving off entirely too much radiation, resulting in shorter live spans. The Hyprobeans went inside this planet. They entered at the polar entrances, inside of where there is another sun which has no radioactive effect. These people still live there in the major city of Shamballa. They are still ruled by the hereditary King of the World. The people who remained on top degenerated into what we call the

Fourth Race.

Q. Did they continue to degenerate?

A. They continued to degenerate. There came to be more differences in the races. They started mental degeneration on the point of warring on each other. Before, fighting was unheard of.

Q. Did they have technology at that time?

A. At that time, the technology was quite high. The Lemurians started in stature from about 12 feet to about nine feet. The fourth race was about nine feet tall. The people started taking on the color of the land. The Atlantean skins were taking on a reddish hue. Asian and Lemurian skins took on a yellowish hue. (Note: Adam means red-man!)

Q. OK, so we had some kind of war going on at that time?

A. Right!...The fourth race. We started to degrade into the fifth race at the time the war started, approximately 25,000 years ago. At this time Atlantis chose to break away from the Motherland Mu. Atlantis was getting more and more vindictive. They were living under the Law of the One—the One God. The Lemurians were the major race at this time which had developed into the Uighers, the Naga-Mayas, and the Quetzelcoatls. The Quetzels at this time started leaving Lemuria in droves.

Q. Where did they go?

A. To North America, then on to the Scandinavian countries. Some of them went south into Central and South America and some of the descendants are still there. Explorers have brought back records of white Indians (true).

Q. Do you know who Quetzelcoatl and Viracocha were?

A. Quetzelcoatl was Venusian. Viracocha was a Lemurian High Priest who went to South America upon the destruction of Lemuria.

Q. What sent Lemuria to the bottom—a war or natural catastrophe?

A. It was the blowing out of Archean gas chambers. When the Earth was forming, huge gas pockets were formed, cavities within the Earth, some of which were just a few feet wide, but thousands of miles long. The scientists started detecting the weakening of the Archean gas chambers on their instruments. This was about 15,000 years ago and at that time the Earth's magnetic field was getting very erratic.

81

Q. Did you have contact with extraterrestrials at that time?

A. At that time we were still in contact with the Federation. Lemuria and Atlantis were both members of the Federation.

Q. Did they have air travel and space travel?

A. Yes, they did. Atlantis and Lemuria could both travel to other planets.

Q. What was it that destroyed Atlantis?

A. After the destruction of Lemuria, which was caused by natural catastrophe, for a long time the planet was unstable, for about 200 or 300 years. The pyramids were built before the destruction of Lemuria. At this time the Atlanteans were becoming difficult and several of them who believed in the Law of the One did not care for what the scientists were doing. The scientists were experimenting with monster crystals that had unbelievable power.

Q. Were there any biological experiments like cloning or with DNA?

A. Yes, there were. This had been going on for hundreds of years by that time. They were using the "things" as their slaves. Some people left Atlantis at this time and came to Mt. Shasta where the Lemurians had built a city called Telos.

Q. Now the Atlanteans started experimenting with huge crystals—were these the fire crystals?

A. Yes, they generated cosmic energy. It is the cut of the crystal which causes the generation (wavelength?). It draws out of the atmosphere (the energy) and generates it into a high force and higher vibration. It has no moving parts. The crystal has an inner fire—they change colors. The crystals the Atlanteans used built up energy they could not control.

Q. Is this the secret of the power source on flying saucers?

A. Yes, a lot of it is crystals, particularly the atmospheric vehicles. The planet-to-planet vehicles are driven by an Ion-Mercury engine. Spaceships can reach speeds way beyond light—they can enter hyperspace—you generate into the fourth dimension—this is controlled by an on-board computer that takes you into and out of hyperspace. I know this is a simplification. When you're on a ship gong into hyperspace, you will hear this vibration and a loud screaming sound when you enter, then you will hear nothing. (I have had many correlations on this data and am researching it further toward a comprehensive theory of space travel).

Q. Do you travel between galaxies?

A. Yes, that is usually when you enter hyperspace when you are going a far, far distance.

Q. Have you heard stories of any advanced beings out there?

A. Yes, they are near the center of the Universe.

Q. What is at the Center?

A. We call it the seat of God—the generation of energy.

• • •

William Hamilton should be congratulated on his being such an energetic and dedicated seeker of truth in this field. He has spent tireless hours without thought of remuneration and has personally neglected any fanfare in order to pierce through the fog of misinformation that is so often placed in our path. Those interested in finding out more about Bill's work can write for information on his privately published manuscript *Alien Magic,* and his group UFORCES. Bill may be reached directly at 249 North Brand Boulevard, Suite 651, Glendale, CA 91203.

Certainly, he is one of those who can testify that the truth will set *us all* free!

Ray Palmer, Richard Shaver and John J. Robinson devoted their lives to discover the secrets of the "Hidden World."

TUNNEL SYSTEMS UNDER US & UFO BASES.

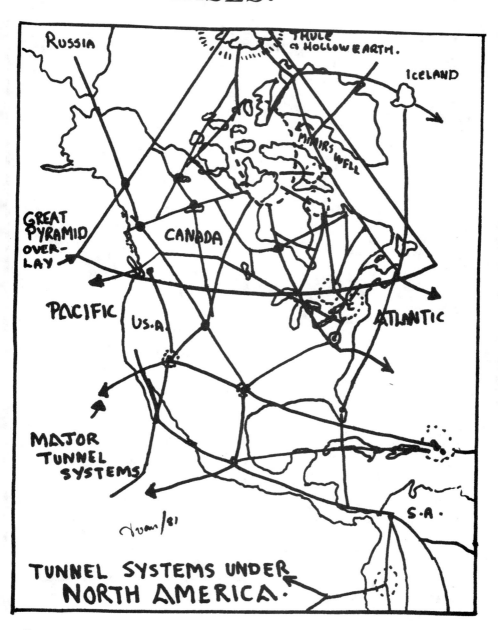

Researcher Ivan Boyes composed detailed map showing ancient tunnel systems under North and South America.

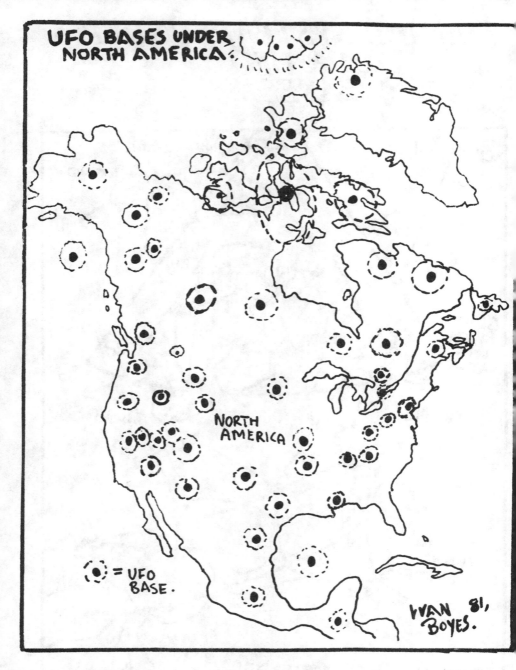

UFO bases under North America according to writer/investigator Ivan Boyes who has had first hand encounters with Dero living under Toronto.

Researcher John J. Robinson talked to one individual who said he saw this being standing guard near a cave entrance.

Brown Mountain

I know of at least one UFO base just about anyone with a car can travel to, and there is a good chance you will see something pretty damn "strange," as thousands of others have over a period of many, many years. The base is in North Carolina. It's in the middle of the Brown Mountain region, and you can stay at the nearby Holiday Inn in Morganton—about 15 miles north of an actual highway marker which has been posted by the state providing any visitor the best view to look and see these mysterious lights that bob and weave across the sky, finally settling down *below* the ground.

There are some who think the lights are a "natural phenomenon," but don't tell any of the locals that, because they know better. A few of them have gotten right up the glowing globes, and they'll swear to you that these things aren't "swamp gas" (besides there is *no* swamp anywhere nearby) or associated with "spook lights" that so often turn out to be connected with mineral deposits in the Earth.

Such things as car lights, or approaching landing lights from planes circling overhead, can also be ruled out, as these lights have been seen around Brown Mountain for several hundred years, perhaps going back as far as 1200. Long before the white man had reached the shores of America, the local Indians reported watching these lights, which roam about the mountain peaks without any "real" explanation.

Various legends have sprung up about the origin of the lights. One has it that the lights are caused by the spirits of the Cherokee and Catawba braves searching the valley for their maiden lovers. It seems that the two tribes had a big battle hundreds of years ago which killed just about all the men of the two tribes. Apparently this legend does have some basis in fact, as most legends do, because within the last several hundred years at least a half-dozen Indian graves have been found in the area nearby.

However, others who have lived near Brown Mountain for as many as 75 years seem to think that there is something even more odd and peculiar than spirits at work in the valley below.

According to Paul Rose, who accompanied us to a secret lookout point despite the 10 degree weather and the falling snow, they may be something from outer space.

Out of all the people living in the area, Rose, and another fellow whom we shall talk about in a minute, seems to have gotten closer to the lights than anyone else. His first sighting came when he was just a youth in about 1916. At the time it was thought that the lights might have been caused by the headlights on locomotives running through a nearby valley. However, during one rough spring all bridges were knocked out and roads were too muddy to enable cars to pass. Yet the Brown Mountain lights were seen, in greater numbers and brighter than ever before, weaving up and down over the trees on Brown Mountain.'

Rose bases his opinion that they are intelligently controlled on the fact that he has seen them fighting, butting into each other and bouncing like big basketballs. He has also tracked them at speeds of almost one hundred miles per hour.

He claims that on one particular night in the late 1950s, when excitement was at an all-time high, two of these lights appeared out of the valley, approached a tower he had built for the purpose of watching them over the trees and climbed to within feet of his position. The next day he, and a friend who had been with him, both became violently ill. This led Rose to the conclusion that these lights are highly radioactive.

Another old time resident of the Brown Mountain area is Ralph Lael, who was born in Alexander county, on a small hillside farm, in 1909. He ran for Congress in 1948 and lost by a few thousand votes. He now operates the "Outer Space Rock Shop Museum" on highway 181, just outside Morganton.

Lael claims not only to have seen the lights up close but to have communicated with them on numerous occasions as well.

Deciding that the only way to uncover the source of these lights was to go into the almost impassable mountain area itself, Lael started his own investigation. Shortly after midnight he got within 100 feet of a light that had risen up from a large hole in the ground. Within 10 or 15 minutes, the first light had been joined by as many as 20 more. Shortly after, they all took off into the timber and disappeared from Lael's view. A half-hour later others began popping up along the mountainside in a smaller valley below. One came so close, within 10 feet, that Lael felt he could have read a book by it.

Several expeditions, and months alter, Lael discovered that by asking the lights questions, they would answer by either moving up

10° planet ?.

and down for yes or back and forth for no. After this form of communicating had been established, one of the lights led Ralph to a door, which leads inside of Brown Mountain.

Once inside he was led to a room about eight feet square, the walls made of crystal "as clear as glass," enabling him to see for what seemed to be miles. Suddenly a voice said: "Do not fear; there is no danger here." The voice continued by saying that Lael has been chosen to tell the people of Earth about their true history; that man was created on another planet named Pewam which our ancestors destroyed. Pewam is now the waste of the asteroids which lie between Mars and Jupiter.

The voices explained that they are not Earthbound beings and cannot eat or drink, but live on Pethine, a "gas we absorb from the light you see around us. We perish in your atmosphere or sunlight."

"We live on Venus, which is a planet of pure crystal as you see surrounding you...notice that the crystal is as clear as your air. Venus is completely surrounded by water vapor about 150 miles above its surface."

In October of 1962 Lael returned to the rock, entered and was offered a ride to Venus—which he accepted. Arriving two days later on Earth's sister planet, he was introduced to men who were said to have been direct descendants of the people from the planet Pewam. One was a rather attractive woman named Noma who was quite beautifully dressed in a bra and panties set.

While on Venus Lael was showed what appeared to be newsreels of the destruction of Pewam as well as scenes going on back on Earth.

Lael was also warned that there are certain "forces" that could decide that man should be destroyed from the Earth. A dial was turned on the wall screen and he was shown how another planet, also the same size as out world, was rendered lifeless.

First he was shown the ice caps at this planet's North and South poles. "Then I saw a great cloud of vapor moving out from the sphere as the waters and oceans began to rush up the mountain sides and into the valleys. Trees were uprooted by the rushing waters, great licking flames of water shot up for miles from the surface of the planet. Much of it remained at great heights as it became vapor. As the picture drew near on the screen, I saw heaps of bodies of some type of animal like our buffalo being tossed around against cliffs of the mountains and higher parts of the valley. As the axis of the sphere seemed to become perpendicular, there was so much mist that I could not see the surface. As the camera or whatever was used to make the picture drew away, the view looked like the planet Venus as we approach it in reverse."

Though Lael was very secretive about this matter, for a long while he kept a "tiny creature," or "little man" that looked "highly preserved" in a glass case in the back room of his roadside Brown Mountain Rock Shop and General Store, which he operated in order to finance his extended trips back into Brown Mountain, where he would "disappear" for weeks at a time presumably to visit with his alien friends in their underground bunker located on the spot.

Lael hinted that this dwarf-like being was actually from some distant world, had died in the area, and had been turned over to Lael because of his love and trust of those not of this place or time.

Although unbelievable as this story may seem, so are the Brown Mountain lights. Ralph Lael told us that "there are many things I have seen and heard that I cannot reveal here because of my obligations to the Brown Mountain lights. Whether you believe or disbelieve what I have told is of no importance. You and others who have read these things should have more brotherly love for the people of Earth and those of the whole universe."

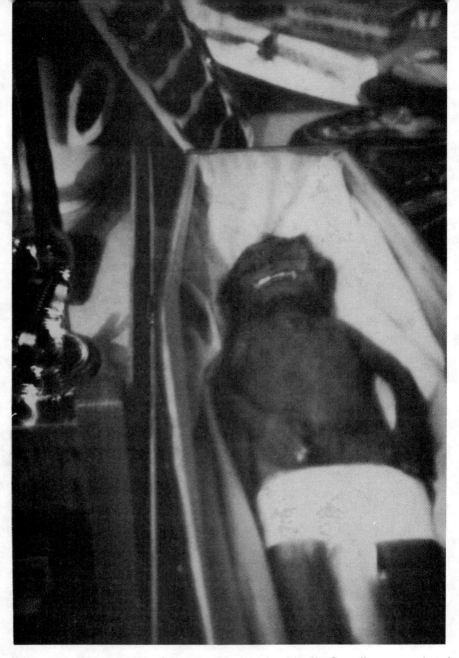

The late Ralph Lael of Brown Mountain, North Carolina, was lead to a UFO base by highly advanced "light beings." In his store he kept a mysterious "little man" in a glass case, whom he indicated he had befriended on one of his trips to "other worlds."

Canadian Saucer Bases

Traveling further North, you'll find any number of UFO bases scattered throughout Canada. Though some of them may be located in the "wilds" from what we hear, there is a stronghold of Dero as well as Greys right under Toronto.

Lake Ontario

If you're looking for proof, my suggestion would be to take a summer vacation and camp out a couple of hours each night on the banks of Lake Ontario. Some pretty weird things have been seen from both the Canadian and American sides. The UFOs seen here are pretty much always the same. They are orange-colored spheres which have the ability to dart across the heavens at incredible speeds, while at other times hover silently like diamonds twinkling in the evening sky. First they shoot from out of "nowhere," and then land for a moment or two on the water itself before submerging into the depths of Lake Ontario. If there isn't an underwater UFO base on Lake Ontario, I'll eat my green beret.

Indeed, the strange behavior on the Lake has convinced several UFO researchers living in the area that the occupants of these craft have constructed underwater bases from which they are free to roam into nearby space without being easily detected. Further proof that these reports should be taken seriously comes in the form of startling photographic evidence—pictures that show bizarre, highly illuminated lights whose origin remains totally unknown at this date.

According to Malcolm Williams, researcher for the Northeastern UFO Organization, infrared photos taken in the dark of night from the shores of Lake Ontario show all sorts of anomalies which cannot be either conventional aircraft or meteorological phenomena. Taken on various occasions, the photos show a pattern of lights in the sky which are definitely under intelligent control as they zig zag about from one position to another in the heavens. One photo shows an object actually resting on top of the water, apparently about ready to make a plunge beneath Lake Ontario.

Many of the photos taken by Malcolm Williams, a former member of the Royal Astronomical Association, were done from a position which would indicate that the main area of interest is over the lake between Oakville and Toronto. This theory is supported by Harry Picken, an aeronautical engineer, pilot and past president of Genair Ltd., a St. Catherine's aircraft research firm. Picken, who owns a home right on the banks of the lake has been keeping tabs on the aerial movements near his property for years. One of the most peculiar things the engineer has noticed is that the lights are usually orange, a color foreign to aircraft lights: "The orange color indicates to me a high sodium content in the light source. Sodium is never used in conventional aircraft lighting," he further points out.

Both Harry Picken and Malcolm Williams believe that the UFO activity over Lake Ontario is somehow related to the fact that a high voltage hydro generating station is located at nearby Lakeview. The UFOs have been seen repeatedly to lift up from the lake and head in the direction of the plant.

Over the years many odd occurrences have taken place in and around Lake Ontario. In his book, *The Great Lakes Triangle,* Jay Gourley tells of several air mishaps in this very locale, adding substance to the theory that something totally "alien" is operating in and around this body of water.

"There is little doubt that the pilot of the twin jet CF-101 Canadian Air Force interceptor, number 18112, knew he was in trouble on August 23, 1954," Gourley states in his well researched reference work on the subject. "He was near Ajax, Ontario, on the north shore of Lake Ontario. He bailed out. He explained later that the aircraft became impossible to control. Publicly, the Canadian Defense Headquarters refused to reveal the cause of the accident. The official cause is classified secret. I have seen this secret file. It says the scientists who studied the case could not determine what caused the jet to become unmanageable." It could be that UFOs utilizing highly magnetized equipment beneath the surface could have accidentally or purposely pulled the aircraft out of the sky.

Lurking Beneath Toronto

Canadian researcher Ivan Boyes is one of the few UFOlogists I know of from this hemisphere who realizes that it may be more profitable to look "closer to home" for UFOs, rather than wander aimlessly out among the stars searching for a solution to this bonifide mystery.

For you see, Boyes has spent a considerable amount of his life probing the enigma of the tunnel system that exists under the Earth's crust. Though others in the UFO field may poke fun at him for unorthodox—to them—views. he has remained determined to root out the problem and confront the enemy below. Some time ago, Boyes filed the following report on what really goes on beneath Toronto, one of Canada's busiest metropolitan areas.

• • •

What do we know of what exists beneath our towns and cities? Not much. Most people think of earth, rocks and eventually dense strata beneath their feet. But is this so? Underneath Toronto, for instance, not all is solid. Vast cave networks have been uncovered by accident in August 1979 by a Torontonian named Ernest. Ernest wishes to remain unknown as to his whole name, but this chap accidentally discovered the cave system that networks under Toronto.

He discovered the cave entrance accidentally when he entered into a small opening off Parliament Street in downtown Toronto, when he was looking for a small kitten he was looking after. The cave was pitch black when he got inside of it and he used his flashlight to see better. There it was with orange and red slanted eyes. It was long and thin, almost like a monkey, three feet long, large teeth, weighing maybe 30 pounds with slate grey fur.

The next thing that occurred according to Ernest was that it said, "Go away, go away," in a hissing voice, then took off down the tunnel off to one side. Ernest took off from there fast as he could.

Many believe that the tunnel was the result of erosion between the apartment buildings here, into the sewer system. But are those tunnels sewers? Living almost directly over the tunnel area, I wonder? For many years before this incident, others and myself have known of a vast tunnel network under Toronto. Not only tunnel systems, but an underground city, deep beneath downtown

Toronto. The city is eons old, built by the El race that once inhabited this area. Vast machines and instruments beyond our wildest dreams exist there. A city of the Gods now abandoned by them ages ago. The center of the complex is under Gerrard Street and Church Street, where still the magnetic machinery is working. A friend and fellow researcher once lived over this site, a Jeff Mitchel. Here strange things occurred that would have terrified anyone else. The pictures on the walls swung around, things moved and other eerie happenings. All result of the effects of the area below. In fact, this corner has the highest accident rate in Toronto. Brakes and vital parts on the cars or motorcycles fail and create fatal accidents, all from the effects of the underground machinery.

The city may not have been inhabited by the ETs, but Deros as well. This fact we discovered the hard way. Sightings of Deros in downtown Toronto at night, evil brown shrewn up faces. One time I encountered one at 4:00 a.m. that had no face except for eyes and two holes in his blank face for a nose breaking area, no mouth at all. Now these Deros have been cleaned out by other positive Inner Earth Beings. The Creature seen by Ernest has been identified by several Oriental Masters as the Sacred Tibetan Kadomma, the Guardian of the gateways to the Cities of Shamballa. They are very positive people, but will destroy negative trespassers.

Legends here of these tunnels are old. The Indians tell of the days far gone by of great saurian creatures coming out of these tunnels and of Atlas battling these creatures. Yes, Atlas, the lord and ruler of the Mound Builders here, according to their legends.

What Was Found in Newfoundland!

If Ivan's story is ripe for an episode of *Tales From the Crypt,* the experience of Arnold White and his friends is certainly worthy of a TV mini series.

Amateur spelunkers, Arnold, Rick and Don came across an underground UFO base while exploring one of the many old iron mine shafts located in Newfoundland Province. This, then, is their very own "weird tale" from the twilight zone of reality.

• • •

Although now generally known, one of these mines—one of

the deepest by the way—had caused much concern and controversy among the local populace. Shortly after it had been dug to its maximum depth, strange things began to happen. Miners working late at night in small groups of six to 10, began hearing noises, not rumbling or other natural mine noises, but what some described as "strange music." It seemed to come from all around them, sometimes faint and sometimes distinct. Later, some said they heard "mumbling" and voices. This went on for several months, but only the miners who heard the noises were disturbed or concerned. Then more serious things began to happen. One of the men entered the mine late at night to check on some equipment, and when he finished and started to leave some "small men" grabbed him from behind, knocked his lamp from his hands and "shot" him with something that forced him violently against the mine wall, knocking him unconscious. In the morning, workers found him apparently none the worse for his experience physically, but quite shaken mentally. He said he would never again enter a mine and promptly dropped out of the occupation.

A few days later a miner on night watch disappeared. Investigators found his lamp and hat deep within the mine, but no trace of the miner. Soon lights and machinery began to fail or work erratically for no apparent reason. Men became hesitant to work the mine. Finally it was "condemned" and shut down.

This was the mine in which our Canadian friend was interested and wanted us to help investigate. Although spelunking is usually confined to exploration of naturally-formed caves, our curiosity was great enough to spur us on to such an unusual form of research.

We arrived in the mining town, which was near the Newfoundland-Quebec border, at 11:30 a.m. on March 22, 1961, and lodged at the local hotel. The next day we got our equipment together, loaded up our jeep and headed for the mine. At the entrance we were stopped by two policemen who warned us not to go inside. When we persisted, they threatened to arrest us. So we left, resolving to return on foot after dark.

At 1:30 a.m. we again set out for the mine. This time we bypassed the police and approached the mine from a different direction. We met no interference along the way and shortly arrived at the entrance.

While Rick Grayton (my American friend) stayed at the entrance as lookout, Don Lawrence (our Canadian friend) and I descended into the mine. It was in excellent shape and showed no signs of any deterioration whatsoever—hardly the type of mine the government would condemn on its physical state alone.

We had just completed our preliminary investigation when we heard someone, apparently deep within the mine, shout in a high-pitched voice, "COME!" We stopped dead in our tracks, and walked in the generation direction from where the voice seemed to originate. Then we heard somebody or something running. We lighted a flare but saw nothing. We continued and again heard the running. By this time we were getting far back in the mine, and also very curious and excited. The running sounds ceased abruptly and we saw a faint blue light radiate from a far recess: Then we heard what we thought was the clank of a metal door closing.

We quickly found the area from which we saw the light radiating, but no door or opening could be found. However, upon tapping the walls with my pick-hammer, we heard hollow metallic reports at several places.

After we had localized the hollow sounding area we marked it off by chiseling off pieces of rock and found that it was generally rectangular in shape, almost five feet in height and about two feet wide. Since we could investigate no further with the equipment at hand, we decided to come back the following night and continue our investigation.

Returning the following night, all three of us entered the mine. Very much to our surprise, the chisel marks were gone! It took us several minutes to find the hollow area again, but we finally did; and this time we had come prepared. Using a battery-powered rock drill, we penetrated about three inches into the rock when we struck metal. We withdrew it and substituted a bit designed to drill into metal. Eventually we breached the metal and, withdrawing the drill, we again saw the soft blue light shining as before. Suddenly we heard a low humming noise and were startled to see the section of the wall we were working on abruptly lift out of sight. It would be an understatement to say we were frightened.

What lay before us was incomprehensible: a blue-lighted corridor which appeared to be made of some sort of translucent, seamless, self-illuminating, blue-colored metal or plastic. At first we were very apprehensive about investigating the enigmatic hallway. Our curiosity soon overcame our fear, however, and we entered the corridor. We had to stoop, for the hallway was only five feet in height. After walking about 50 yards we came to another corridor leading off to our left and decided to explore it. We reached the end of the corridor after walking about 100 yards. There we encountered a steep, spiralling stairway. We descended it for at least 20 minutes, all the while noting that the lighting was becoming more brilliant. Finally we reached the bottom and were confronted with yet another corridor, this one light green in color.

After a brief rest we set off down that corridor. It was only about 100 feet long, and we traversed it quickly. To the right and left were oval entrances. Making a quick decision, we decided to enter the one on the right, and noticed immediately that it was cylindrical-shaped and much larger than the previous passageways. It contained a floor on the same level as the previous ones. We also noted that this passage was evidently made of some crystalline substance, and that a bright, but soft white light emanated from it. It curved downward at a slight angle.

We next came to a huge chamber which appeared to be some type of scientific laboratory and hydroponic garden. In one section were rows of giant exotic plants and in another some type of chemistry equipment. Lining the walls of this laboratory were arrays of multi-sized TV screens, dials, gauges, and other electronic equipment. Some of the screens were at least 10 feet square. In the center section was a great mass of scintillating vari-colored crystal; it had a rough, natural exterior and apparently performed some unknown function. The rest of the chamber contained many other strange devices and apparatus that none of us could identify. The entire ceiling was one great light. At its far end stood something that looked like a car lift, with a disc-shaped metal object resting on it. We decided to take a closer look at it.

Fortunately the lift was only about two feet off the floor and we got a good look at the object. It was circular in shape, about 35 feet in diameter and four feet in thickness. Suddenly Don exclaimed, "It's a Flying Saucer!" We both agreed—we had indeed found a "UFO." Rick stepped up on the lift to take a more detailed look at the saucer. He tapped on it lightly with his hammer and parts of it sounded hollow. Immediately after he tapped on one certain spot, an entire section of its tail dematerialized. This took Rick totally by surprise and he almost fell off the lift platform. About one half of the inner mechanism was revealed to us, and again we could not find a single piece of equipment with which we were familiar. The only thing we could surmise was that the object was a remotely-controlled device, since there was no space provided for passengers that we could see. Rick jumped down from the lift and we continued our investigation of the laboratory.

Abruptly the lift was activated and began to drop to the floor, and at the same time the lighting in the chamber changed from a soft white to a deep red. In short order, the screen directly above and to the right of us flashed on. Due to the unnatural lighting we could not make out the image on the screen. Then we heard a voice from the screen.

It said (in a high-pitched voice): "You have been expected. You have been observed since first you entered our domain. You gaze upon the upper regions of our world. You are the first of your kind to be permitted this privilege. Let it be known this truth—we harbor you no ill will; we depend not upon your superficial world for our sustenance or pleasure. Those of your kind who make themselves the interpreters of our intentions are naught but the picayunish deceivers of your civilization. Let it again be said that we desire man no harm and wish only to pursue our independent existence on this, our mutual planet. We shall not influence nor bring to you discord in any medium. We are not doers of evil. Our world spans the inner gulf of your globe; we have existed since before your time. Had we wished harm upon you we would also have been its receivers. We beg you a friendly farewell and hope our message will be heeded and find wide acceptance among those of your kind who find it necessary to concern themselves with our domain."

The screen then faded, without our having seen a clearly defined image of the person who had spoken. Luckily, Don had quickly written in his notebook what the voice had said to us.

The red lighting in the chamber suddenly became even deeper in tint and all of us felt light-headed. Rick shouted he was going to faint and started to fall, but we caught him. Then we too had the same feeling and blacked out.

When we regained consciousness we found ourselves lying outside the mine entrance. We still retained our personal effects: notebooks, pencils, wallets, etc., but all our equipment, such as

100

safety hats, pick-hammers, and chisels, and our Geiger counter, had disappeared.

After returning to the States, Don found all the pages of his notebook "burned" or charred, as though it had been thrown into a roaring fire. The notebook cover, however, which was made of plastic, was surprisingly undamaged. All of us had worn wrist watches with radium dials. Some weeks later the radium became inactive and the dials no longer glowed in the dark.

Artist Gene Duplantier indicates his belief that UFOs are using underground bases as a "way station" while visiting our planet.

Flying Saucers From the Earth's Interior

I don't know where Dr. Raymond Bernard is today. Chances are that he may have gone to visit his friends inside the Earth and decided to stay in this paradise beneath our feet.

South America is full of tunnels and underground UFO bases. Flying saucers are an accepted part of life in Brazil, where Bernard made his home for many years, turning out a number of important books that many of you are probably familiar with, such as *Flying Saucers From the Earth's Interior.*

Atlanteans From the Inner Earth

Of all the countries on the face of the Earth, none other is more mysterious, or less explored, than is Brazil. Miles upon miles of this country have never been set foot upon by white men. In these areas live wild tribes of savage Indians whose civilizations are said to be akin to those existing at the time of our Stone Age. Many of those who have dared venture into these pockets of unexplored jungle have never come out. Perhaps the case of Colonel Fawcett will be familiar to readers as an example of what I mean. He supposedly was captured by a tribe of wild Indians while in search of a "hidden city" said to be located within the confines of the dense jungle. However, according to the late Dr. Raymond Bernard, he may actually still be alive—living in a vast underground city built by the descendants of Atlantis.

Before his death, Dr. Bernard had sent this writer many personal letters regarding his findings related to this underground civilization. We quote from these communications in the following:

• • •

103

I arrived in Brazil in 1956 and have been carrying on my research since I met a Theosophical leader who told me about the subterranean cities, inhabited by a super race of Atlantean origin, that exist in Brazil. He referred me to Professor Henrique Jose de Souza, president of the Brazilian Theosophical Society, at Sao Lourenco in the state of Minas Gerais, who erected a temple dedicated to Agharta, which is the Buddhist name of the Subterranean World. Here in Brazil live Theosophists from all parts of the world, all of whom believe in the existence of the subterranean cities.

Professor de Souza told me that the great English explorer Colonel Fawcett is still alive, living in a subterranean city in the Roncador Mountains of Matto Grosso, where he found the subterranean city of Atlanteans for which he searched, but is held prisoner lest he reveal the secret of its whereabouts. He was not killed by Indians as is commonly believed. Professor de Souza claimed he has visited subterranean cities, including Shamballah, the world capital of the subterranean empire of Agharta. I then went to Matto Grosso to find the subterranean city where Fawcett is claimed to be living with his son Jack, but failed to do so. I then returned to Joinville in the state of Santa Catarina, and there continued my research.

Just recently two of my explorers returned from entering a tunnel near Ponte Grosse in the state of Parana. One of them had recently entered alone and spent five days in the underworld city there. It had about 50 inhabitants plus children. The fruit orchards were recently planted, and the inhabitants received fruit from another subterranean city. During the last visit, the two explorers were met at the entrance of the tunnel by a guardian and the chief of the city, who told them that they should return in two years when the fruit trees will start to bear, but cannot enter now.

These same two explorers entered a tunnel near Rincon, state of Parna, and finally came to a chimney-like structure with four chains hanging down. They descended on the chains but when they came near the bottom a gas with a chemical odor started to come up and forced them to ascend. Obviously the subterranean dwellers tried to keep them from reaching their city. [Editor's Note: This seems often to be the case.]

Our explorer J.D. [name on file], who is a mountain guide of the Mystery Mountain near Joinville (where there is supposed to be

104

an entrance) said that, several times, he saw a huge luminous flying saucer ascend from the tunnel opening that leads to a subterranean city inside this mountain, in which he heard the beautiful choral singing of men and women, and also heard the "canto galo" (rooster crowing), a universal symbol indicating the existence of subterranean cities in Brazil. He said that the saucer was so luminous that it lit up the night sky and converted it into daylight. On one occasion he met a group of subterranean men outside the tunnel. They were short, stocky, with reddish beards and long hair, and very muscular. When he tried to approach them, they vanished. Often he saw strange illuminations in this area at night which were probably produced by flying saucers. (We use the name "Mystery Mountain," rather than reveal the true name of the mountain, so that unwanted outsiders will not come here to locate it.) Throughout my many years of research I have accumulated a vast amount of data which would indicate that these entrances to subterranean cities abound throughout the region.

An elderly man living in Joinville once told me that he had visited a tunnel near Concepiao in the state of Sao Paulo, and saw in the distance a marvelous subterranean city with vehicles darting back and forth, evidently traveling through tunnels from one subterranean city to another.

Although the following report requires confirmation, it was told to me by an explorer named N.C. who said that he had visited a tunnel near Rio Casdor and had met a beautiful young woman appearing to be 20 years of age. She spoke to him in Portuguese and said that she was 2,500 years of age. He also met a bearded subterranean man. Still another explorer named D.O. visited this same tunnel and saw a child inside, who fled upon seeing him. Also as he once lay in front of the tunnel opening, a man with a beard and long hair passed over him and entered.

Another explorer visited a similar tunnel near Gaspar, Santa Catarina, and behind a wonderful fruit orchard saw a subterranean woman with a child in her arms reading to it aloud from a huge book written in an unknown language (Atlantean). After she read each sentence the child repeated the same and in this way was taught how to read. All of these subterranean cities are illuminated by strange light.

Dr. Bernard told this writer that although he had himself never been in such a city, he had met the Atlanteans on various occasions on the surface and had heard their singing and strange illuminations (coming from underground) a number of towns.

A number of years ago, the late Ray Palmer (editor of *Flying Saucers* and *Search*) received a lengthy signed letter from a man residing in Joinville who claimed to have found Shaver's caves. He was shown their settlement only because he was a descendant of the Incas who have been sworn to secrecy. His letter to Mr. Palmer is reproduced below:

•••

Inca

I am descended form the Inca race, which disappeared in a tunnel when the Spaniards invaded their country, and continued to live in subterranean cities. The Incas were a race of vegetarians and pacifists, and when the Spaniards came to attack them, they did not fight, but escaped into tunnels and disappeared from the world.

Brazil tunnels

During all my life I have been searching for my lost race and traveled to many countries, as far north as Mexico, also in Venezuela, Chili, Paraguay, Argentina, Uruguay and all parts of Brazil, investigating tunnels to find an entrance to the subterranean world. But I could not find anything, and lost (through swindlers claiming to bring me to Atlanteans under the Earth) and spent 1,800,000 cruzieros, equivalent to $36,000.

After my money was gone, I worked as a mechanic and saved money and with it, I continued my investigations. After searching all the 21 states of Brazil and living a year in Matto Grosso among the savages, I finally found what I sought.

One day I went to a river to drink water. On the other side was a high mountain. I heard a powerful voice coming from the top of the mountain, yelling many times. I thought it was a person lost in the forest and asking for help. I swam the river to the other side and walked through the forest an hour and then climbed for two and a half hours. When I reached the top I found a hole in the ground. It was very deep as I found by dropping a stone down. I then gathered vines from trees, tied them together, fastened a stone at the end and dropped it down until it hit bottom. I pulled it up and it measured 100 meters or 328 feet.

Then I returned to Joinville and told Dr. Raymond Bernard about this, who gave me money to buy a rope. I returned to the mountain and by means of the rope I descended. When I came to the bottom I entered a tunnel which I traversed for a distance of 2,000 meters. I then saw with my flashlight a door of stone. While I was watching the door, it suddenly opened and I saw a very tall man with a metallic outfit, who spoke with a powerful voice and said that this was the first time that anyone had the courage to enter the tunnel. I was first frightened at the powerful voice of the man and wanted to run, but he called me and told me not to be afraid as he was a very peaceful person who never did harm to any living being. So I asked him who he was to live in this cavern. He said, "I am an Atlantean-Inca, the guardian of this door." He asked me what I was looking for. I told him I was looking for my race, because I too am an Inca. He seemed to be very pleased to hear this. I told him I would like to visit his city, and that I had an American friend and a wife, who would like to go there, too, with my children. He told me to bring photographs of my wife, children and American friend, and if they were found acceptable, he would give permission for them to enter.

I then returned to Dr. Bernard, who gave me his own photo, and I brought all the photos, including those of my wife and children, back to the Atlantean.

On this second visit to the Atlantean he delivered a lecture on radioactivity and its danger. He said that radioactive dust in the air is now causing surface dwellers to age very rapidly because it accumulates in the pores of the skin and stops skin respiration. He said the pores of the skin have a constant alternate contraction and expansion and serve to take in air and expel foreign matter. In an atmosphere of radioactive dust metals, these substances clog up the pores and interfere with their vital functions of respiration and excretion. This causes disease and early death.

The Atlantean called me to come near a transparent screen to make an exchange of blood to make sure I will preserve the secret of the whereabouts of this tunnel, so that I do not reveal it to an unworthy person. When I was near the curved plastic screen, another curved plastic screen suddenly appeared from each side of the

107

door and encompassed me, so that I found myself inside the two curved plastic screens. Then it seemed that all air was pumped out, leaving a vacuum in the space where I was between the plastic screens. Then other air entered, which seemed lighter and purer, which made me feel more healthful and stronger. Then the inside plastic door opened, and he put me inside a man-sized capsule of this transparent substance which he held by handles on both sides of it, and told me to go inside the open door. After I was inside, the door automatically called.

Now the second plastic door opened and the Atlantean took hold of the handles on each side of the capsule and carried me to the other side of the inside plastic screen whose door automatically opened and shut.

Then he inserted his hands into two soft pockets in the capsule, made of the same material and took hold of a metal device which he lowered on the chain and wire with which it was suspended from the curved top of the capsule (the base was flat for me to stand on) and put it on my head. Then he went over to a recording apparatus, from which a recording tape emerged and I heard a ticking sound, much like a telegraphic ticket. Then he read the tape, put it in a box and spoke in a funnel-shaped speaker in a strange language. It seemed to be a radio telephone.

Then he asked me for the photos. He told me to put my hand by one part of the capsule with a very delicate wall. He told me to push my hand through, which I did and the material adhered to my hand like an elastic, so as not to permit any air from inside the capsule to leave, since he was afraid of my having contaminated the air inside the capsule by which I exhaled. Then he sprayed my hand with a purpose of radioactive decontamination. He took the photos from my had and slid them into an opening in the same electrical apparatus. Then more tape emerged, which he read and then spoke by radio telephone to headquarters below. He then looked at a sort of small television apparatus with a horizontal screen, apparently to see the persons he was speaking to.

He told me not to bring any unworthy person, because he would know it in advance. I asked how. He said that with this apparatus, which he called an "electrovisor," he could behold whatever was occurring in any part of the world. If any unworthy person comes near the mountain and tries to get to the tunnel opening, certain rays confuse the person's mind, so that he is unable to continue the trip and will go off in a wrong direction.

I had some bread in a pocket. He told me not to eat the bread. He put a white pill in my hand (which was projected outside the capsule all the time), and told me this pill had the taste of many fruits and that his people lived entirely on it. I believe it was a concentrate of fruits. Then I withdrew my hand and the elastic material through which it projected closed.

After he gave me the pill he carried the capsule with me inside to the space between the two plastic screens, as the door of the inside screen opened to admit the capsule and then automatically shut. Then the door of the capsule opened, I left the capsule, and then the door of the outside plastic screen opened and I left.

When newcomers enter, they first enter the capsule, and the Atlantean carries them to a Decontamination Chamber (the Atlantean told me). The door of the capsule opens, the person leaves the capsule, takes off his clothing, then the chamber becomes filled with vapor which draws forth radioactive poisons from his body. The person dressed with other clothing there ready for him, then enters an "electronic apparatus," which carries him to the center of the Earth. I should mention that during my visits, before the door opened I heard a peculiar humming sound, which was of the apparatus with which the Atlantean came up from below, which became louder and louder as the apparatus came near, and when it came to a stop the noise stopped and the doors automatically opened. I should also mention that when a flying saucer came near my house on Saturday, June 13, 1959, in the afternoon and night, it gave off a hum identical to that of this subterranean apparatus, which makes me think they are both operated by the same mechanism and that the flying saucer was an apparatus of these same subterranean Atlanteans and did not come from another planet. The flying saucer came describing a spiral, descended to the top of a hill about 2,000 meters from my house, and then rose in a spiral manner, with a tail of light behind it. It came in the night, had a round shape and a silver color.

• • •

Apparently such tunnels into the subsurface exist elsewhere in the world besides Brazil. In fact one letter on file with us comes from Professor W. Wiers of Mexico, who tells us that he knew Professor Schwartz, who had made a long study of cave problems, starting when he was only 15 years old in Germany. According to Professor Wiers, just before the beginning of the Second World War, both the axis and allied powers were interested in using various caves as supply bases, and for many military applications.

Professor Schwartz at one time had stated that he knew of a Nazi who had come upon an "enormous circular Pit" whose sides dropped straight down for a good 1,200 feet. Trees could be seen growing tall and straight below. Eagles soared around, and then dived to the center of the bottom, apparently to eat something. Since the sides were dangerously steep the Nazi had to content himself with using binoculars instead of descending into the world himself.

Returning later with others he eventually discovered a similar but much narrower bore, or shaft, not far from the first, which was so big that it could not be hidden in anyway. Not having cable or apparatus with which to let down a man in the seemingly bottomless shaft, they let down a pencil attached to a rope. To their surprise, the cord, when drawn back up was found to be cut clean, as with a knife, or scissors—and the pencil was gone. Of course they all resolved to come back to study this put further but the war prevented their doing so.

The location of this shaft is supposedly in Northern Guatemala. Near the place is a witch doctor, friendly to Professor Schwartz, who assured the professor that there is a secret passage, closed by a revolving rock door, which goes to the still enormous chamber which is still below the vast roof cave-in seen from above.

As we pointed out earlier, in many of these cases there seems to be an overt attempt by the subsurface beings to keep their existence unknown at any cost. Those who do happen upon their civilizations, or tunnel entrances, seldom are released to tell anyone about them.

According to our West Coast correspondent, Cosette Willoughby, there is an area in Africa also inhabited by Atlanteans. A big game hunter reportedly heard about a plateau in a remote region where White Gods, who never died, were said to dwell. Since the region was taboo to most of the natives who lived at the foot of

110

the Plateau, the hunter, perhaps craving excitement, decided to make a trip into the area and see for himself what truths there were to these stories. The trip turned out to be quite hazardous, but he finally arrived at the Plateau and found the natives there quite friendly, though primitive. The day after his arrival he decided to get close to the plateau and take pictures. But when he tried, a shower of iron balls (like cannon balls) rained down upon him and he barely escaped with his life.

• • •

Dr. Bernard wrote extensively on the form an interior world beneath the surface might take. I quote extensively from the personal papers he provided me through the years:

• • •

It is claimed that there once existed an advanced civilization on the prehistoric continent of Atlantis, whose scientific development was beyond our own, and that their air vehicles, known as "vimanas," were identical with what we now call flying saucers. This great civilization destroyed through a terrible nuclear war which brought on a terrible geological catastrophe and a flood. Prior to its total destruction, certain better inhabitants of Atlantis escaped by flying in their flying saucers into the hollow interior of the Earth through the polar openings, where they continued to live on ever since. These Atlanteans are a race of giants; and their final war is referred to in mythology as the war of the Titans. Michael X writes:

"I believe that Atlantis was every bit real, and that the Atlanteans' Ancestors are living today, now, in the interior of the Earth. They are all probably very large people, physically. Perhaps blonde giants. But why believe they are still in existence?

"Because persistent rumors have it that a vast system of subterranean *tunnels* exist beneath the land of South America. Secret openings are said to exist, leading from the surface of the Earth into the tunnels. In his book *Agharta,* Robert E. Dickhoff claims that a fantastic network of tunnels exists underground. According to Dickhoff, one tunnel surfaces in the Motto Grosso region of Brazil, precisely where Colonel Fawcett vanished in 1925. Perhaps he found the 'secret city' and more. A tunnel nearby leading down into the Earth's fantastic cavern kingdoms, and maybe the people there never permitted him to leave." (This is the opinion of Commander Paulo J. Strauss and Professor H.J. de Souza.)

We quote from a letter from Ottmar Kaub: Writing about the book, *The Smoky God*, by Willis George Emerson, he says: "This book has the books of Reed and Gardner all beat. I read it through at one sitting and was never so excited in my life. The Smoky God is the inner sun. It is supposed to be the true story of a Norse father and son who, with their small fishing boat and unbounded courage, attempted to find the land beyond the North Wind as they had heard of its warmth and beauty. A miraculous storm and wind carried them most of the distance. They spent two years there and returned via the South Pole and the father lost his life when a berg broke in two and destroyed the boat. The son was rescued and subsequently spent 24 years in prison for insanity when he told the true story. When he was released, he told the story to no one, but after 26 years as a fisherman, he saved enough to retire in this country, coming to Illinois and then to California. In his 90s, by accident, the novelist, Willis George Emerson, befriended him and was told the story; on the old man's deathbed, he relinquished the maps that he had made of the Inner Earth and the manuscript. He refused to take chances while he lived, due to his past experience in having people disbelieve him and consider him insane to mention it. (*The Smoky God*, by Willis George Emerson, is published by Inspired Novels.)

"Olaf Jansen claims that the four rivers of Genesis (Paradise) are very large and flowing in the Inner Earth, and much gold was there as Genesis states. The rivers are larger than the Amazon. Jansen checked all the explorers, as Reed and Gardner did later on, and Emerson has this material quoted briefly, but proves all the points about the Inner Earth. *The Smoky God* is a masterpiece based on arctic reports...."

Michael X, in his book referred to above, quoted Dr. Nephi Cottam of Los Angeles, who said that one of his patients, a man of Nordic descent, told him the following story:

"I live near the Arctic Circle in Norway. One summer my friend and I made up our minds to take a boat trip together, and go as far as we could into the North country. So we put one month's good provisions into a small fishing boat and with sail and also a good engine in our boat, set out to sea.

"At the end of one month we had traveled far into the north, beyond the pole and into a strange new country. We were much astonished at the weather there. Warm, and at times at night it was almost too warm to sleep. Then he saw something so strange we both were astonished. Ahead of the warm, open sea we were on was what looked like a great mountain. Into that mountain at a certain point, the ocean seemed to be emptying. Mystified, we continued in that direction and found ourselves sailing into a vast canyon leading into the interior of the Earth. We kept sailing and then saw what surprised us—a sun shining in the Earth!

"The ocean that had carried us into the hollow interior of the Earth gradually became a river. This river leads, as we came to realize later...all through the inner surface of the world from one end to the other. It can take you, if you follow it long enough, from the North Pole clear to the South Pole.

"We saw that the inner Earth's surface was divided, even as the outer one is, into both land and water. There is plenty of sunshine, and both animal and vegetable life abound there. We sailed further and further into this fantastic country...fantastic because everything was huge in size as compared with things on the outside. Plants are big, trees gigantic, and then we came upon the GIANTS.

"They were dwelling in homes and towns, just as we do on the Earth's surface. And they used a type of electric conveyance like a monorail car, to transport people. It ran along the river's edge from town to town.

"Several of the inner Earth inhabitants—huge giants—detected our boat on the river, and were quite amazed. They seemed just as astonished to see us as we were to see them! They were, however, quite friendly. We were invited to dine with them in their homes, and so my companion and I separated—he going with one giant to that giant's home, and I going with another giant to his home.

"My gigantic friend brought me home to his family, and I was completely dismayed to see the huge size of all the objects in his home. The dinner table was colossal. A plate was put before me and filled with a portion of food so big it would have fed me abundantly for an entire week! The giant offered me a cluster of grapes and each grape was as big as one of our outer-earth peaches. I tasted one and found it far sweeter than any I had ever tasted "outside." In the inner Earth all the fruits and vegetables taste far better and more flavorsome than those we have on the outer Earth.

"We stayed with the giants for one year, enjoying their companionship as much as they enjoyed knowing us. We observed many strange and unusual things during our visit with these remarkable people, and were continually amazed at their scientific progress and inventions. All of this time they were never unfriendly to us, and we were allowed to return to our home in the same manner in which we had come—in fact, they courteously offered their protection if we should need it for the return voyage."

Dr. George Marlo claims to have made this same trip many times by flying saucer, and has met the people living inside the Earth's crust and is known to them. He described the people as being 12 to 14 feet tall. The men have short beards. He speaks of choirs of 25,000 people. The men wear sandals and shorts. He speaks of musical instruments, especially harps. He speaks of grapes as large as oranges and apples the size of a man's head. He mentions five cities, named Eden, Nigi, Delfi, Jehu and Hectea. They speak a language like Sanscrit (probably Atlantean). He said they marry at the age of 75 to 100 and live for 600 to 800 years of age. He speaks of birds with 30 foot wingspread, which lay eggs two feet long. He mentions tortoises 25 to 30 feet long, and elephant-like creatures (resembling those which emerged from the North Polar opening to be frozen as mammoths); and penguins nine feet tall. He speaks of trees 1,000 feet tall and 120 feet in diameter. He said that the compass inside the Earth points north and leads one to the South Polar opening...."

The following are reports told the writer in Brazil concerning Inner Earth people and flying saucers. There is no proof at all that these reports are true. They may be lies invented by the narrators in order to create an impression. But whether true or false they are interesting and show along what lines people are thinking today.

A Russian who formerly served in the Russian army said he and his troops once reached Lhasa, Tibet, where he was stationed some time, and there he came in touch with a secret society of Tibetan vegetarians who made regular trips by flying saucer through the North Polar opening into the hollow interior of the Earth. He says he saw the saucer that made these trips. He said that the supreme object of all Tibetan lamas and yogis is to prepare their bodies to be worthy to be picked up by a flying saucer and carried to the hollow interior of the Earth, whose human population consists mostly of Tibetan lamas and Oriental yogis, and very few Westerners since Westerners are too bound to the things of this world, while lamas and yogis wish to escape from this miserable world and enter a much better world in the hollow interior of the Earth.

The reason why subterranean people sent their flying saucers to us after the Hiroshima atomic explosion in 1945 was because they were afraid that further explosions might poison the air that comes into their interior atmosphere through the polar openings, coming from the outer air.

This contactee describes flying saucers as made of a brilliant nickel that glows with a light at night. He says that the people of the Earth's interior wield a form of energy beyond atomic energy (electromagnetism) which motivates their flying saucers. They use this superior energy (the "vril" of Bulwer Lytton) only for peaceful purposes.

Also these people have one government and one nation and are not divided into warring nations as we are. This is helped by their speaking all the same language. They are in advance of us in all ways. They live without religion as we know it, obeying the laws of nature, which they consider better than believing in religion and supernatural gods and saviors, while disobeying nature's laws in our daily lives, such as by eating meat, indulging in sex, etc. These people are vegetarians and live in complete chastity.

Robert Dickhoff, in his book *Agharta,* mentions that the secret chambers of the Pyramid of Gizeh were connected by tunnels with the Subterranean World. An Egyptian informant says that at the base of this pyramid are three tunnels that radiate in different directions. Two lead to dead ends, but the third seems to go on and on and may have once connected Atlantis with its colony in Egypt by passing under the Mediterranean and Atlantic. Two Swedes tried to traverse this long tunnel till its end and never returned. While believed to have died, rescue parties could not find them. This caused the government to forbid anyone from entering this third long tunnel, though they were permitted to enter the other two. There are strange reports of ancient Egyptians (or Atlanteans) having been seen inside the long tunnel, coming from the Subterranean World.

Many believe that the Swedes who disappeared joined these people. A popular book was selling in Egypt some time ago entitled *The Mysterious Path to the Unknown World,* dealing with the apparently endless third tunnel below the pyramid of Gizeh and the world to which it leads.

As Donnelly points out in his book *Atlantis the Antediluvian World,* the pyramids, with their four sides and truncated top, memorialize the sacred mountain of the gods in the center of Atlantis from which their builders came. It is probable that the messengers from the Subterranean gods traveled on swift-moving vehicles through the tunnels that open at the base of the pyramids.

A report has been circulating that some scientists entered a tunnel in West Africa that ran under the ocean bed in the direction of the vanished Atlantis, which was finally reached and many mechanical contrivances were then seen on the ocean bed, including motor vehicles. How true this report is, the writer cannot say. Another report refers to the discovery of a subterranean city by Brazilian scientists, reached by a tunnel opening near the border of the states of Santa Catarina and Parana. Similar subterranean cities were reported in Motto Grosso, whose entrances are guarded by fierce Chavantes and Bat Indians.

After three years of searching in Brazil for an opening to the Subterranean World, the author has come to the conclusion that it is not necessary to search for the subterranean cities of the Atlanteans in the Roncador Mountains of Motto Grosso as Colonel Fawcett did, since the states of Santa Catarina and Parana, Brazil are honeycombed by a network of Atlantean tunnels that lead to subterranean cities. The writer is now organizing an expedition known as the Aghartan Expedition, for the purpose of investigating these tunnels, with the object of reaching the subterranean cities to which they lead, after which he hopes to establish contact with the still-living members of the Elder Race of Atlanteans and arrange for bringing qualified persons to them to establish residence in their cities in a world free from fallout and thus avoid a radioactive destruction which will eventually be the fate of all surface dwellers.

Space Brothers Set Up "Mystery Zone" in Brazil

Investigators have long marveled over the extent and variety of UFO activity that has made Brazil the South American capital of the flying saucer world. So many cases have transpired in Brazil over the years that it would take a full length book to do the subject justice. Just as an example, any researcher worth his salt would have to mention, at least in passing, the following incidents:

• The abduction—and subsequent seduction—of Antonio Villas-Boas, who apparently had sexual relations with a full-blooded space woman. *(Are this photogin L ?)*

• An aerial "attack" made on Fort Itaipu, a military base, in which two sentries were badly burned and all the lights went out after a UFO flew over the installation.

• The explosion of a disk-shaped device over the coastal town of Ubatuba in which fragments of the destroyed craft were collected and analyzed; proving to be the best "physical evidence" case on record to date.

• And last, but not least, a close encounter at sea, in which a Saturn-shaped craft was photographed from the deck of the Brazilian Navy training ship *Almirante Saldanha* just off the coast of Trindade Island, resulting in a controversy that has lasted to this day.

Today, as everyone else, UFO reports have persisted and even increased in number. In addition to the usual number of confrontations with aliens, actual communication (usually of a telepathic nature) also seems to have broken out, keeping up with patterns set in the rest of the world.

One of the more active groups keeping track of all UFOlogical action is headquartered in Colonia. The GOPU (short for Grupo Operacional de Investigaciones OVNI) is made up of students and professional people, including professors of physics and astronomy. Interestingly, they also are assisted by psychics and those whose backgrounds lay in the area of parapsychology.

As far as anyone can recall, the first inkling of anything unusual happening in San Fidelis was over 10 years ago. A farmer was awakened at around 4:00 a.m. by a bright light which paraded across the sky and was said to have resembled a Hat. San Fidelis is located in district 40, about 200 kilometers from Rio de Janeiro, and is mainly a rural area with a population slightly over 5,000. The locals are hard working ranchers and farmers who don't have time for nonsense. They work from dawn to dusk to feed their families and UFOs are far from their mind.

Baffled

During December, 1981, investigators from GOPU found themselves camping out in this community. They had come at the request of residents who were baffled and admittedly frightened by an event which had transpired toward dawn. The heavens were filled with a brilliant glow and suddenly there was a violent explosion that rocked the area. Many thought that an airliner had crashed in the mountains just outside of town. A rescue party was quickly organized but they could find no signs of a wreck. But what they did discover puzzled them immensely. The ground in one particular area was flattened out and was "bald," all the vegetation having disappeared. The organization got together all the witnesses they could find and interviewed them at length. They were amazed to learn that UFO reports in the area were previously unknown. Ten years ago, as an example, at about 4:00 a.m. on a hot summer morning a 65 year old farmer, Aristao de Sousa, left his home to go to work when he observed a bright colored light moving along at a rather high rate of speed. He said the object resembled a "hat" and its colors changed several times during the period it was visible.

Coming to the conclusion that something "mysterious" was happening in the area the GOPU called in a local psychic who has been able to demonstrate paranormal powers since he was a child. Supposedly, Hilario Pinto Machado has predicted earthquakes and foresaw the tragic death of the president, Castelo Branco. He even states that he was able to cure his dog of rabies after the local vet had said it would be impossible to treat the animal. Hilario, so the story goes, had fallen asleep deeply depressed over having to kill his pet. In the dream he brought the dog medication from the drug store. The dog got well the very next day and still lives with the psychic.

Machado went into a light trance in front of the team of investigators and started to channel a space being by the name of Guivizan who claimed to be the commander of the space fleet responsible for the UFO activity in this area. When questioned about the event they had been called in to research, Guivizan claimed they had cleared the ground of vegetation by using ultrasound. During their encampment near the site, they requested through the UFO contactee that the Space Brothers put on a demonstration, so that they could confirm that the messages were valid ones.

118

After much insistence, Guivizan replied: "So you are skeptical and want to se our craft? Well, then, here it is!" Moments later, everyone present saw a "star" approaching rapidly. It was illuminated in blues and greens and orange. The UFO did a strange sort of dance which included bobbing up and down. Members of the GOPU rushed to their cars to fetch their photographic equipment, but the peculiar object vanished before they could set up their equipment.

The Investigation

In March, 1982, the group returned to this rather isolated spot in order to conduct further investigations. Among the things that their research showed was that the area was full of minerals. Several scientists in GOPU put forward the theory that somehow the mineral deposits in the mountains made it possible for the aliens to establish telepathic contact with earthlings more easily than otherwise would be possible.

This time the GOPU came very well equipped with portable radios, tape recorders and a special device which could detect any magnetic force fields around the camp. Roberto Santos, the physics professor, who is very knowledgeable in electronics strung up a system of red and blue lights which he said would blink on and off at a set frequency.

Aurelio Zaluar, a reporter, who covered the GOPU investigation, filed this report with the paper *El Mundo:* "I decided to stay near the equipment, a rather short distance from the top of a rock where the others had gone.

"Visibility was rather poor being that it was cold and drizzling. Dark clouds obscured the sky. We had been at this locale close to a day when suddenly the magnetic meter that had been strung up began to beep. At that same instant our walkie-talkie came alive. On the other end was Vanderlei Penna, a lawyer and a long time member of the GOPU. He suggested that we climb to the area of the rock where other members of the group were experiencing 'strange things.' Immediately, I started out from the camp with a companion. We had been told to take a certain short cut but decided against this route because it took us through a thicket full of spiders and perhaps even snakes. It was dark and raining and all we had to light our way was a flashlight which soon went out anyway.

119

"When we reached the summit, we called out and Vanderlei Penna came forward warning us to keep our voices down. His outstretched finger pointed toward the shadowy figure of another member of the group. Luis Otavio de Silva Carvalho, a young lawyer, stood motionless with his hands clasped over his ears. He was heard to cry out and plead in anguish, 'Don't speak, don't make any noise, my head can't stand any more.'

"As we stood there in total amazement an unknown aerial object was seen about 500 meters over the mountains. In front of our very eyes it stopped over what is known as "Warm Water Falls," a waterfall that remains warm even in the middle of winter.

"Luis was still acting up and we were told to join hands and think peaceful thoughts so that the spell over him could be broken. All at once he fell to the ground and we picked him up. Soon he regained consciousness and was anxious to know what all the fuss was about. We explained the situation to him and little by little he seemed to understand, complaining of a bad headache.

"After a drink of water back at the camp his head cleared further and he told us what he alone had seen. Luis was standing near some of the equipment when he saw a glowing figure materializing in front of him. It was about four feet tall, had long hair and was wearing brilliant clothes. He said that soon there was a whole score of these beings who were all moving about at the same time. He remembered that when I had extended my hand, my arm cut right through one of these beings. He said that right over us, very close, was a large triangular-shaped ship with colored lights on top. Luis was the only one who saw all of this. The rest of us only saw the strong light which moved around in diverse directions at the summit of Warm Water Falls."

Interestingly enough, reporter Zaluar concluded his story by saying that the group broke camp around two o'clock and descended to the base of the mountain. The first house they passed happened to belong to a farmer who had been up all night and was in his pajamas. "What happened up there on the mountain?" he wanted to know. "Why?" responded the reporter. "Because my heart was pounding, I felt ill and I had a premonition that something was happening up there!" At the time he had no way of knowing just how right his psychic premonition had been.

As late as June of that year, sightings were still being made in the area. One rancher, Francisco Pereira Duarte, a 65-year-old father of two and grandfather of seven, said it was approaching dusk and he was returning home carrying a sack of feed, when in front of his ranch he saw a very luminous object. It changed colors several times and the light from it was so brilliant. that it hurt his eyes. He was frightened but did not run away. Instead he followed the direction of the light which he thought looked like a "luminous cart." Repeatedly the "cart" would accelerate to incredible speeds and would disappear only to reappear somewhere else in the heavens. To him, it was an awesome sight.

At this time the Brazilian group GOPU plans further work in the area. They hope to eventually come up with conclusive documentation that the sightings around Colonia are valid ones. Like their American UFOlogical counterparts they are beginning to see that more than a pure scientific background is necessary when investigating this enigma. It takes a variety of researchers versed in many different areas, including that of the psychic and parapsychologist. Brazil, it would seem, has often played host to visits from the Space Brothers, and there is every reason to believe that they will return in the near future.

Rainbow City—
Capitol of the Underworld

Inside the Earth at the South Pole is said to exist an ancient center of culture called "Rainbow City," which currently is in the hands of reincarnated descendants of the first colonizers from outer space who made tropical Antarctica the "Mother Land of the World" some two and a half million years ago. There also exist six other cities (all connected by vast underground tunnels), completely dormant, while "Rainbow City" is protected on all sides by warm hot springs. However, to prevent its being discovered and exploited by outsiders, ice walls some 10,000 feet high have been built around the city so that it can be reached only by those who know its exact location.

Rainbow City was first discovered in 1942 by Emery (his last name has been kept secret for good reasons), a professional musician still active today in certain theatre circles with the help and assistance of a group known as "The Ancient Three."

In a privately circulated text (until now restricted to a very few) Mr. and Mrs. William Hefferlin, formerly of San Francisco (now believed to be living in Rainbow City with 2,000 other people), describe Emery's first visit as follows:

Emery guided the ship down into the park belonging to the temple at Rainbow City. There was sufficient room between the huge trees for him to maneuver the ship safely. He was amazed to see the high structures, before him, towering into the air, and capped by a pyramidal structure, whose base was the same size as the Temple. Lights were shining on the outside of the Temple and in every street from the Temple Plaza.

As Emery and the small group with him moved to the Temple, they were not sure that their eyes were clear. For everything was a conglomerate mass of colors used in the plastics, which made up the streets, the buildings, and the Temple. There were bright reds, screaming oranges, and violent purples too—but sparingly. The predominant colors are the softer, more subdued tones. All in all, the effect is not at all harsh, but is very pleasing.

The group entered a door set at ground level in the Temple hall, which opened onto a short flight of steps, that led down into an anteroom, which was below the first floor level of the Temple. This in turn led to a large room which had carved upright pillars, tables with what appeared to be lamps upon them. Books were lying on the tables and other books were stacked in racks. There were chairs placed about at various tables. Everything was of larger than normal size, indicating that the people who built these things were around eight feet tall at the least.

Over at once side of the room was a huge chair-like thing with great arms, with what appeared to be keyboards covered with queer characters set into the arms. Hanging from a hook, on the back of the chair, was what appeared to be some form of book. The back of this chair towered high into the air, and there was a strange bucket-like cap, that was set in upright slots, so that it could be raised and lowered over the sea. From this sliding piece and from the foot-rest, many strands of wire were gathered into cables, which went into a wall behind what seemed to be a control board. For it was covered with knobs and levers and pointers, on what seemed to be graduated dial faces. Soft, artificial light glowed in the room, casting no shadows. There was nothing in the dark in that room—everything was fully illuminated.

Emery and those with him had touched nothing as yet, for it was all too unknown at the moment. Yet curiosity drew them on.

Emery examined one of the lamp-like affairs, but he found no indication of a switch or button. The base was set firmly into the table so that it could not be moved, or it was exceptionally heavy. Emery put his hand on the shade of the lamp and it turned very slightly under his hand. He pushed harder, and a stream of clear brilliant light fell in a circle upon the tabletop right over the book that was lying there. He opened the book at random and a voice issued from the book, speaking in an unknown language. The pages were covered with strange characters and as the voice continued speaking, little lights illuminated groups of the characters, then passed onto the next group. With the rhythmic voice speaking and groups of characters being successively lit up, Emery surmised that the voice was speaking the words of the text. Later, he learned that his surmise was correct.

When the lights had illuminated the last group of characters on that page the voice ceased, not to be resumed until the page was turned. Closing the covers of the book also caused the voice to cease. These volumes became known as "The Talking Books."

After this Emery began to examine the pillars. Upon the first was carved a representation of the Solar System, with the third and fourth planets in colors—the third green and the fourth red. Leading from the red planet was a group of elongated dots, and other marks, that looked like pointers headed toward the base of the green planet. On the same pillar was series of markings (straight lines) in arithmetical order; after each group appeared a character evidently depicting the numeral system. There were circles divided into different ways and characters in relation to them. There were squares and triangles and cubes with different sets of characters following.

Also on the same pillar were a group of characters, the same kind which appeared in the Talking Book. That was evidently the alphabet.

Close by the pillar was a table with many piles of books upon it. Comparing the characters on the plastic with the characters of the counting system, Emery discovered that each pile of books was numbered in arithmetical order, beginning with Number One. Inasmuch as it was vitally necessary to learn the language, so they would be able to understand the many things there in Rainbow City, Emery, as leader of the expedition, set everyone to work studying the books in the first pile. The group soon progressed through Number 14, known as "The Book of Zo."

The first books were silent, but they were definitely primers in the way they were compiled. There were the separate characters which were used in forming the words. There was a picture of the Solar System, and it had its name. The various planets were pointed out, each with its name. Then a single house with its name, and another term below it. There were other structures with a name attached to each, and the same under each. Emery judged that the specific name for the structure was the first one; then the general term under which the structure of various kinds were grouped.

There were many other nouns pictured and names. Then they turned to the verbs. Pictures of action and its equivalent term under each picture. There were also simple arithmetic problems, such as addition tables, each with simple marks showing the addition, and what they counted; then the symbol that represented that group number.

When they had finished with the first set of books, they went over to the second set. These were duplicates of the first books, but with the one addition of voice. The alphabet was repeated—each letter repeated several times by voice and illuminated at the same time. Then the simple numbers were sounded, and the simple addition tables, simple subtraction tables. Is it any wonder that we have said elsewhere that the city had been left in preparation for a return of Mankind some day?

Fortunately for Emery he had a knowledge of a number of European languages, as well as a knowledge of Oriental. He discovered that the root words of certain sacred Asiatic languages were basically the root words of this ancient language of Rainbow City, and this made it easier to help the others learn. The talking books gave them pronunciation and inflection, and led into other books that were more technical, and much deeper in many subjects, and their time in Rainbow City has been so very short. After the group had studied quite a way in the books, they read the instruction book on the chair-like machine, then followed them. They each sat in the chair, with hands fastened down on the arms. The huge cap was lowered over the head, and the power turned on. This machine sent a gentle vibration throughout the brain and nerves. They found that later they could continue the learning of the language with greater ease and flexibility in speech. Also that their comprehension of the contents of the books was greater.

Growing in the center of the city are giant shade trees and flowering plants, luxurious beyond belief, whose individual blooms measure at times as much as three feet in diameter. Plastics are used for the walls, floors and roofs of all the buildings composing Rainbow City. "The homes and all buildings are heated or cooled by heat or cold radiations from the walls and floors. The very color of the dwellings can be adjusted through a change in the color vibration control and the walls either become opaque or transparent as desired, by adjusting a switch in the wall."

The main structure, towering far above all others, is Rainbow Temple, where all the knowledge of the ancient races is stored in great libraries and museums. "The libraries are so arranged that they are accessible to the laboratories above them..." In the top of the Temple there are fully equipped laboratories and every possible facility for research in electricity, chemistry, and all other known sciences.

Other rooms have been constructed for worship and hospital facilities. One of the noted physicians to make the journey in 1942 was supposed to have been at one time the Court Physician at the palace in Budapest.

Most of the walls in the Temple are "elaborately decorated, whether carved or molded we do not know. But the plastic is extremely hard and tough. All heat is radiated from the walls, floors and ceiling. There are no light fixtures, as light, too, is radiated from the walls, ceilings, and floors. A simple push on a button chooses the kind of light that is desired. In here there is no difference between night or day, because one has the choice of choosing that particular light. This same light source seems to revitalize the air and act as an air conditioner as well. Draftless, shadowless, peace and quiet is here for rest and relaxation, study or contemplation, thought or concentration."

The outside of the Temple can be reached from all avenues of the city. All buildings in the vicinity are two and one-half stories high. Then "two stories high, and as one goes farther from the temple, one story high. Close in near the Temple there are buildings stocked full of all things, similar to our present day retail stores. Here in this city there are no apartment houses or tenements, no crowding; each house has a spacious lot for flower gardens and greens."

We are also told that all of the heavy industry was carried out in the underground city of some five levels surrounding the Temple's basement. Also underground there are stores, workshops and houses. Sunlight does not exist—since the city is not exposed to the sky—but is simulated by special light equipment. We are told by the Hefferlins that "The saying, often referred to in history, 'that there were giants in the Earth in those days,' could well have applied here, for everything is of larger than to us normal size."

Some of the electrical equipment found in the Temple was utterly fantastic. In fact, one room was in itself a television viewer which could be set to tune in on the past. And also by setting the viewer in a certain fashion and entering a door in the "viewer room" it was possible to teleport one's self to any location on Earth. The name for this door was "Portal" and we are told that "Mythology, folklore and religion seem to give some hints to substantiate these Portals, and we must consider that mythology and folklore as well as religion are but a resume of the past." One example which the Hefferlin's quote in their text is that:

"Vulcan made for the Gods the golden shoes with which they trod the air, or the water, and moved from place to place with the speed of the wind, or even thought."

The Portals can also be used to transport supplies and man from various locations to other places. "These same Portals will reach out through local space to the Moon, but not much farther at present."

Other legends have it that an ancient Serpent Race built similar cities millions of years ago and that they have hibernated in special capsules with the plan in mind of eventually conquering the earth.

In his book *My Visit to Venus,* the legendary T. Lobsang Rampa tells of visiting Rainbow City and meeting there the Masters from the planet Venus. These beings were the "ancient wise ones" whose telepathic abilities are keenly attuned and are able to move through space via the power of the mind. They are also able to live for hundreds of years in near perfect health.

There are reports that remain under great secrecy—according to my military sources—of expeditions mounted to explore these strange lands. But, the realization of all of these myths and legends that have been handed down through the centuries must await further exploration and review of the evidence of those who have gone in search for the truth—and have returned!

ALSO BY
COMMANDER X
THE ULTIMATE DECEPTION

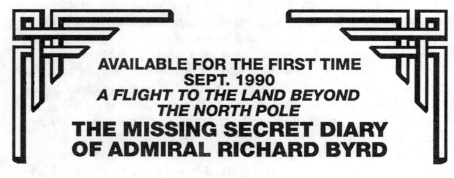